DRIVE TO SURVIVE!

CURT RICH

MBI Publishing Company

First published in 1998 by MBI Publishing Company, 729 Prospect Avenue, PO Box 1, Osceola, WI 54020-0001 USA

MBI Publishing Company books are also available at discounts in bulk quantity for industrial or sales-promotional use. For details write to Special Sales Manager at Motorbooks International Wholesalers & Distributors, 729 Prospect Avenue, PO Box 1, Osceola, WI 54020-0001 USA.

Library of Congress Cataloging-in-Publication Data
    Rich, Curt.
        Drive to survive/Curt Rich.
           p. cm.
    Includes index.
    ISBN 0-7603-0525-0 (pbk.: alk. paper)
    1. Automobile driving. 2. Traffic safety. I. Title.
    TL152.5.C87   1998
    629.28'304—dc21   98-44887

Cover design by Tom Heffron

Printed in the United States of America

CONTENTS

Acknowledgments   4

Introduction
  Combat Survival Techniques for the Road   5

Chapter 1   Jeff Cooper's Color Code
            A Guide to Situational Awareness   12

Chapter 2   Combat Concepts for the Road   17

Chapter 3   Avoiding the Dumb Accident   22

Chapter 4   High-Performance Driving Techniques
            for the Road   40

Chapter 5   Avoiding the Crazies   65

Chapter 6   Evasive Driving Techniques   72

Chapter 7   Kidnapping and Carjacking   101

Chapter 8   Defeating Murphy   116

Chapter 9   Putting It All Together   125

            Index   127

ACKNOWLEDGMENTS

Thanks go to several people for assistance with this book. Jeff Cooper and Massad Ayoob read for content. Mad Mac Atteberry assisted with photographs and his medical and rescue expertise. Sam Woolf, an experienced member of a big-city SWAT team, kept me straight on some esoteric technical points. Peter Dayton, an instructor at Lethal Force Institute as well as a friend, added his expertise. And lastly, my red-headed traveling companion did her usual expert job of proofreading and making my work more readable, not to mention her modeling skills and putting up with me spending all of my spare time on the project for the last year.

INTRODUCTION

COMBAT SURVIVAL TECHNIQUES FOR THE ROAD

> *I am sending you out like sheep among wolves.*
> *Therefore be as shrewd as snakes and as innocent as doves.*
> Matthew 10:16

In 1969 I went to war. I didn't want to. I wasn't warrior material, but I had little choice. The Army had paid for the last years of my schooling, and now it was payback time. I found myself, at age 23, an Army captain, dumped into a year of combat. After six months of combat I had a rear-area job for two weeks, but I was soon sent back to the field to a recon unit for punishment. I was not cut out to be an REMF during a war. (An REMF is a military term for those guys in the rear with beer; the first two words are Rear Echelon.)

I knew going in that you could get killed in combat no matter what you did. One of Murphy's Laws of Combat is "Anything you do can get you killed, including doing nothing." I am now quite familiar with all of Murphy's Laws of Combat. But I assumed you would improve your odds for survival if you just didn't play John Wayne. But I saw people get killed because of the stupidest things:

• One Vietnamese soldier killed one of his buddies and maimed himself and several others fiddling with a blasting cap we had captured from an enemy cache.

The author as a very young Army Captain. Forced to learn combat survival techniques, he learned quickly and remembered what he learned. According to statistics, driving is about the most dangerous thing most of us do, so why not use the same techniques and the same mindset where it's appropriate?

Rallying isn't supposed to be a water sport, but flash floods happen. In this 1991 SCCA National Championship rally in Missouri, the road became flooded. Despite this, Rich and his ace navigator, Debbie Rich, went on to win the event. A good rallyist excels at situational awareness, precision driving, and concentration.

- An American lieutenant colonel walked into a helicopter blade trying to hurry after his much shorter Vietnamese counterpart.
- A young lieutenant and his sergeant were killed by a mine when they rode their Jeep down an unsecured, unswept (by mine sweepers) dirt road to a nearby town. They just wanted to go into the town. They weren't going on any military mission.
- A major failed to unload a captured Chinese K54 (Tokarev TT33) pistol before cleaning it. Apparently he dropped the magazine and thought it was unloaded, failing to check for a round in the chamber. The K54 is not equipped with a safety. He shot himself in the abdomen and died before the medevac helicopter could land.

Unfortunately, I could make the list much longer. Those are just a few examples.

Having people trying to kill you makes you a fast learner. Learning by experience is usually fatal in combat. You have to learn by the experience of others. I learned fast. Most combat survivors did. There was some luck involved, of course; there always is. I was very lucky. But I developed a survival-oriented mindset. I don't mean I hid in the rear. I couldn't if I wanted to (and I often wanted to), because the job involved being on the sharp end. But I developed the skills of a jungle fighter.

Well, it's still a jungle out there, Jane. When I came home I noted a

Autocrossing is an affordable way to go racing with the car you need to drive to work Monday morning. Cars go through the course one at a time, so damage is rare. Rich won two regional championships in his daily driver Mercedes-Benz 190E 2.6 Sportline. Autocrossing teaches and tests precision driving techniques and concentration.

lot of combat veterans were dying in automobile accidents, especially the first few months after returning. This was nothing new: Automobile accidents have been a significant cause of death since the invention of the automobile. Before that, men and women, boys and girls died in horse-and-buggy accidents. My great-grandfather died in a buggy accident in his thirties. One of his uncles died at the age of 12 when he fell off the covered wagon, and a wheel ran over him.

Some number of automobile accidents are inevitable, and perhaps some are even unavoidable, though I've never seen one I would consider unavoidable. Some were probably unavoidable by one of the people involved, but not by both. They all involved a screw-up by one or more people.

But I don't want to go that way; it seems like such a waste. If someone in combat died doing something noble, such as rescuing wounded, it was tragic, but we felt a little bit better about it than if he had walked into a helicopter blade or run over a mine on a run to town. I figured then if I had to go, I'd rather do it in a way that the guy writing the letter to my folks wouldn't have to lie. And I conducted myself accordingly—most of the time. As it turned out, I had several close calls, some scratches and minor wounds, but I survived to come home.

Along the way I began to develop combat survival techniques for the daily automotive combat. I honed my driving skills just as in combat I honed my shooting skills. I was an "advisor" to Vietnamese troops. During one period I would put out road security teams every morning, and if the bad guys didn't attack a convoy, we had nothing much to do. My radio operator and I fired up a case of M-16 or .45 A. C. P. pistol ammunition a day for most of a month. More than once I survived by outshooting the opposition. I also became an expert at the other skills of an infantry officer in combat by necessity. I could calmly and accurately call in artillery or helicopter fire or tactical aircraft with precision on targets so close that any errors on my or the pilot's part would mean

SCCA racing, the ultimate in a precision, high-stress, high-speed driving challenge. Concentration and the ability to do exactly the same thing with an automobile every lap are the keys.

friendly casualties. Since we virtually never could make contact with the enemy unless he outnumbered us, this was necessary for survival. Calling fire "Danger Close" became a way of life.

Back in the United States, I reactivated my interest in motorsports, autocrossing and rallying, honing my driving skills. I attended high-performance driving schools. Over the years I've sat in the car with Bob Bondurant, Bill Buff, Johnny O'Connell, John Paul, Johnny Unser, John Rutherford IV, and a whole lot more I'll probably insult by forgetting, and with guys not so well known but quite capable of turning a car around on a one-lane dirt road at 35 mph or of knocking a pursuer into the weeds or escaping pursuit by the hounds of hell in a faster car. They know, and appreciate not being mentioned by name. There are policemen I should mention, but considering the political nature of police chiefs, I won't, and thus they won't ever have to worry about standing in front of a new chief explaining why they gave me aid and comfort.

I had always, like most of us, disdained the techniques of teaching used in driver's education in the early sixties. The instructors tried to scare us to death. If you're scared to death of something, you try not to think about it. If you try not to think about it, you're unlikely to spend the time honing your skills at it. So I won't be trying to scare anyone here. If I do, it's not intentional.

Driving has always been fun for me. I've spent a lot of my time doing it. I became SCCA National Rally Champion twice before retiring a grand master of the sport: someone with more than 200 lifetime

One Lap of America, an annual tour of racetracks around the country. Cars drive 5,000–6,000 miles around the United States and drive time trials at 10 to 12 racetracks. Here the author drives at the Road America racetrack during the 1994 event. All driving and road survival skills are tested there.

points, the equivalent of winning 20 national rallies outright. In doing so I drove 30,000 miles a year, crossed the United States countless times, and drove in as many as three rallies in a weekend. I remember driving once from San Jose, California, to Hutchison Beach, Florida, for a rally, in 40 hours—in a fairly low-performance car. I autocrossed to more than one regional Solo II title, and the trophies I had won, when I finally cleaned them out, filled up a 4' x 10' storage room. I ran One Lap of America, a 5,300-mile, six-day-and-night run through 10 racetracks for time trials. I tried SCCA racing and became an instructor for the Porsche Club of America, teaching people how to lap Texas World Speedway quickly without falling off the track.

Along the way, in addition, I became an avid shooter, taking up IPSC (International Practical Shooting Confederation) practical pistol competition. Practical pistol competition is shooting matches designed to simulate real gunfights. No, the targets never shot back, or I assure you, I'd have been somewhere else. I've been shot at all I care to, thank you. But the matches simulated real gunfights in that you had to shoot fast, from a holster, and against realistic targets, sometimes with no-shoot "hostage" targets interspersed among the "bad guys." During my peak I shot in two IPSC matches a week and practice-shot 1,000 rounds of pistol ammunition a week.

In my search for training in the sport I met three remarkable teachers who teach gunfight survival for police, military, and carefully selected civilians: Jeff Cooper, Ray Chapman, and Massad Ayoob. I spent multiple weeks with Jeff and Ray at their respective schools and became real friends with Jeff, attending several courses at the American Pistol Institute (later Gunsite Training Center) at Gunsite Ranch in Arizona, learning the pistol and combat shotgun. From Jeff I learned The Color Code and the Principles of Personal Defense. I applied them to driving as well. From Ray I learned a lot of shooting techniques, such as shooting from a moving vehicle, and shooting at moving targets. I never made it to one of Massad's courses (despite several attempts gone awry), but I read a lot of his prolific writings and talked to him a lot and corresponded. From him I learned to quantify the effects of stress on the body and how to counter them or live with them, and I learned the legal aspects of self-defense from him. He is one of the content readers of this book.

Jeff Cooper's operations manager when I first went to Gunsite, Clint Smith, now has his own facility, Thunder Ranch, in the beautiful Texas Hill Country, and he has contributed to the book, too.

Because more and more the dangers of automobiles aren't limited to traffic accidents, necessary survival skills aren't limited to driving skills. Now people are getting kidnapped from parking lots, or carjacked (a word that didn't even exist when I grew up), or just plain robbed, often with fatal results. The lack of punishment for crimes in the United States has turned the land of the free and the home of the brave into a very dangerous place.

During all of this I made a living in the car business, in the luxury end for most of the time. My clients were worried about being carjacked or robbed in their garages, and some were. Some were shot at. Others were run off the road or chased or harassed without cause. So I became involved in their problems and in helping them protect themselves.

The purpose of this book is to give you a start at the tools and techniques to become a "combat master" of the most dangerous thing you're likely to try, driving an automobile in the United State and enable you to have fun doing it. This is not like driver's ed. It's O.K. to have fun driving. It's O.K. to drive fast, as long as you do it safely. It's O.K. to have fun on back roads. It's not O.K. to get maimed or killed or to do so to someone else.

I do warn you I will try to teach you when to walk away from a fight (and when to run), but I will also teach you to fight back when it is appropriate. If you don't believe in the right of self-defense—and some people don't—you won't get as much out of this book. But read it anyway. You might change your mind when the shooting starts, and you might remember something.

Once in Vietnam, I was sitting at a helipad at 93rd Evac Hospital in Than Son Nhut waiting for a helicopter to take me back to the war. Waiting with me were two other soldiers. One was a Protestant chaplain who had just earned the Silver Star for heroism in combat when the patrol he was accompanying was in contact, and the young lieutenant in charge was killed, and the chaplain had taken over and rescued the platoon. The other was a young enlisted man. Since we had a long wait for the helicopter, we struck up a conversation. The young troop said he wasn't into Christianity. He was into Zen, and he didn't believe the Army had the right to order him to kill people. The chaplain said, "Son, the Army doesn't order men to kill people. However, they do train you well, arm you with a weapon, and put you in a position where someone might be trying to kill you. When you get in that position, you can choose to defend yourself . . . or not. It's your choice. The Army has faith that you'll do the proper thing."

In this book, I'll try to give you the basics and tell you where to get more training, and life will put you in a position where you might need to defend yourself, and then it's your choice, too.

CHAPTER ONE

JEFF COOPER'S COLOR CODE
A GUIDE TO SITUATIONAL AWARENESS

It's a hostile world out there. People are being carjacked. They're also being shot at, sometimes with no apparent provocation. They are being robbed in parking lots and in their garages. Drivers on the road are becoming more and more aggressive, less caring or aware of the effects of their actions on other drivers, and thus far more dangerous. They're still becoming involved in accidents, particularly the "not-at-fault" accident. We all know people who have had an accident every year or so but, "I wasn't at fault. They gave the other guy the ticket." Other people never have accidents, not even the "not-at-fault" ones. They survive unscathed in an increasingly dangerous environment of heavy traffic and hostile drivers ignoring the rules of the road or actively trying to harass other cars.

Why? What's the difference between them and the poor guy with the black cloud over his head who gets in an accident a year? It's probably the difference between an ace fighter pilot and his latest victim. Assuming the schnook with a poor accident record of "not-at-fault" accidents isn't a drunk or on drugs (not necessarily a safe assumption), it's probably situational awareness.

The key to survival in any hostile environment is situational awareness, how to know what's going on around you. Ace fighter pilots are masters at this. They might be upside down and pulling six Gs, but they know where up and down are and where all the friendlies and enemy are.

When I was living in the jungle—the green one, not the concrete one—I developed this sense. I learned how the jungle sounded, smelled, and looked. If the noise of the animals, birds, and insects changed, I knew there was a reason. I could observe this when down in the dirt at ground level. When in an armored vehicle this was impossible, and armor units pretty much went from ambush to ambush—as the ambushee. Infantry soldiers, if they were to survive, learned this awareness. They learned to scan their sector in a consistent manner. They learned to concentrate, to look for things out of place, things that didn't belong. The jungle was full of booby traps, enemy soldiers, dangerous

Jeff Cooper, a retired Marine Lieutenant Colonel, invented the Modern Technique of the Pistol and revolutionized firearms tactics. His Color Code for situational awareness has saved countless lives.

animals, insects, and even plants. You either learned to master it, or it mastered you. If it mastered you, you were unlikely to survive.

There is a system designed to teach situational awareness. It's called the Color Code. I learned it at a place called Gunsite Ranch in Arizona. Gunsite was founded by an ex-Marine Lieutenant Colonel, Jeff Cooper. Jeff sold the school and now teaches rifle and pistol courses at the NRA Whittingon Center in New Mexico several times a year.

Jeff teaches what he calls "Crisis Management in short-range interpersonal confrontations." This is legalese for surviving gunfights. He teaches a lot of government employees such as Marine marksmanship instructors, Navy SEALs, and Army Special Forces, and the legalese helps make the course acceptable to government funding agencies. What he teaches is valuable not only in gunfights, but for surviving in any hostile environment.

If you are going to survive, the first thing to learn is how to stay alert so no one sneaks up on you and you get a chance to react to potentially dangerous situations. Being alert means having a high level of situational awareness. An easy way to classify levels of alertness is by learning the Color Code. The Color Code is a system that assigns four colors (white, yellow, orange, and red) to increasing levels of situational awareness.

Condition White

Relaxed, unaware of your surroundings. Everybody's been there. If someone ever ran into you, and you didn't see it coming, you were in Condition White. If someone sneaks up on you, you're in Condition White. Most people who die violently die in Condition White. (Even in combat, I saw ambush victims who never knew they were in danger until they were already dead. Erich Hartmann, the greatest ace fighter pilot of all time, said most of his victims never knew he was in the air with them.) You see people there every day. They're looking out of the car just enough to drive down the road, but their minds are somewhere else, inside the car, maybe 1,000 miles away. Or maybe they're just tired, dead tired.

Incident 1

Many women get their cars stolen from them at gunpoint outside shopping malls near Christmas time. During fall and winter of 1990, a Nigerian gang was stealing luxury cars in Houston in this fashion. They hired junkies to steal the cars for them. The victims came out of the shopping mall in Condition White. They didn't see their assailants until it was too late. Had they been in Condition Yellow, described below, they would have seen something was wrong, and they would have done something about it, such as going back inside and looking for a security guard.

Condition Yellow

Relaxed, aware. This should be your perpetual condition when you're driving. You know what's around you on all four sides, and you know what other cars are doing. At traffic lights you don't just go when the light turns green, you hesitate that split second to make sure all the lanes on the left are clear, and that all the cars approaching the intersection from the sides are stopping. Then you quickly cross the intersection to minimize your exposure. In a local crash, a driver was hit and killed by a speeding garbage truck that ran a red light. It should be noted that the garbage truck driver was totally at fault legally, but of course that doesn't matter. Three days after it happened I hesitated a split second at an intersection with poor visibility to the left, perhaps with that on my mind, and a speeding garbage truck went through the intersection at 50 mph. I crossed, found a place to pull over, and pondered my mortality.

It takes little effort to be in Condition Yellow, and if you practice it for a month, it'll become a habit. If you're in Condition Yellow, no one will ever follow you home, and no one will sneak up on you in a parking lot because when you come out of the store you'll look around and become aware of your surroundings.

You can make a game of it. Every day, whenever a car "sneaks up" on you (and I put "sneaks up" in quotes), give yourself one demerit. By that I mean whenever you go to change lanes, and there's a car in your blind spot, give yourself one demerit (assuming you don't hit him, which earns a lot more demerits). Whenever you look in the rearview mirror, and there's a car there you didn't know was there, give yourself one demerit. During your free time make yourself work off the demerits by giving up something you want, whether it's a gin and tonic before dinner or your favorite dessert. You'll wind up either sober and skinny or alert. Note that there's no way to get "merits." Being alert one day doesn't make up for failing to be alert another. You get only one chance at each situation, and if you're in Condition White when the grim reaper goes trolling, then he's going to get you, no matter what you did the day before.

It probably goes without saying that drinking and driving prevents you from getting into Condition Yellow. A drunk driver is in the ultimate Condition White. A driver who is not drunk but has had a drink or two cannot exercise sufficient alertness to be in Condition Yellow. For those who think they can have a drink or two with dinner and drive at 100 percent, I recommend finding a child's Nintendo game and play Super Mario Brothers until you're good at it. There is a point in the game where the window for survival by jumping over a mine cart is very small. Get to where you can successfully negotiate that, then have one beer. You will safely see the results of your diminished reaction time. As one father told me, "You're toast. There's no way you can survive. It made a believer out of me."

Condition Orange

Specific alert. You see the car ahead of you weaving. The car behind is approaching too quickly. The aforementioned garbage truck is approaching the intersection at flank. Consider these vehicles dangerous and watch them. Don't let them hurt you. You think a car is following you. Make three right turns. If he's still there, he is following you. If you see someone near your car in the parking lot go back inside. Watch him. Wait until he leaves or call for a security guard.

Look for the abnormal. Jeff likens it to a pawnbroker who sees a man come into his store wearing a coat on a 90-degree day. The pawnbroker stands next to the alarm button, maybe with his hand on the pistol under the counter. If the man opens the coat to reveal a sawed-off shotgun, the pawnbroker can handle it. If, instead, he wants to pawn the coat, that's fine. The pawnbroker can relax back to Condition Yellow. In Condition Orange you are actively looking for avenues of escape. You are looking for cover. If you were armed, you would put your hand on your weapon. It will certainly be close at hand.

Condition Red

Mental trigger. Attack in progress. Fight or flight. The garbage truck isn't going to slow down. If you enter the intersection, you will die. The proper reaction is to stop. The man in the coat reveals the shotgun. The proper reaction might be to shoot him, carefully, until he loses interest in shooting you for the contents of the cash register. If the car has followed you through three right turns, don't go home. Go to a police station, a fire station, hospital emergency room entrance, even a full-service gas station, lacking anything else. If you have a car phone, call the police, of course. It is virtually impossible to go quickly from Condition White to Condition Red, but very easy to go from Condition Yellow to Condition Red. In over 38 years of driving, I've seen a lot of Condition Reds, from drunks and druggies behind the wheel, to a crazy with a gun, to bandits in automobiles, to a lot of lethally poor drivers. So have you. If you're in Condition White, one of them will get you sooner or later. You have an 86 percent chance of being in a major automobile accident during your lifetime.

Living in Condition Yellow isn't difficult, and training yourself to do so is very easy. Take a grease pencil or magic marker and write on the rearview mirror of your car *yellow* and today's date. If you have a yellow magic marker, you can just put a dot on the mirror in yellow. You'll know what it means. If you look at it every day for a month, it'll become a habit. After a month you can wipe it off if you want to. I learned this from a man who forced himself to wear seat belts using this simple reminder method. On the other hand, nothing says you *have* to wipe it off. If, on a bad Monday morning when you're running late and deep in Condition White because your mind is on what will happen if you're late to work, or on how to make it to work on time, you see the yellow dot on the mirror and just think, "Oh, Condition Yellow," then you'll make it to work all right; maybe not on time, but all right.

CHAPTER TWO

COMBAT CONCEPTS FOR THE ROAD

One of Murphy's Laws of Combat is "Anything you do can get you killed, including doing nothing." In combat (and for the purposes of this book, all life is combat), there is no guarantee you'll survive even if you do everything right. (If you keep doing things wrong, however, you'll definitely draw the short straw.) There are three elements, known as the Combat Triad, which will increase effectiveness and survivability in combat and on the road.

1. The Combat Mindset

When I arrived in Vietnam I did not have a combat mindset. I didn't want to be there and would have preferred a job in the rear. But that was not to be, and I was assigned to replace a lieutenant who had been killed in an infantry advisor's job. I was taken under the wing of two second-tour sergeants, and they started telling me how things *really* were, not like they had been in training. One gave me an army parachute knife. This might not sound like much, but it had a huge effect on me. A parachute knife is a switchblade knife with a second hook blade for cutting shroud lines. Every boy who grew up in the fifties and sixties knew that a switchblade knife was a mark of evil. Gang members carried them, and the government made them illegal. This very experienced sergeant thought I might need this item in the course of my tour. I was in a job in which my performance could be enhanced by the possession of a switchblade knife. What would my mother think?

This came as a shock, but I took it to heart and decided that if my job involved such a level of savagery in a time when men were walking on the moon, I'd better take it damn seriously. In the course of the next year I would see men die who did not take it seriously. I listened to everything the sergeants said. They suggested several items of nonissue equipment. Instead of the heavy and uncomfortable web gear issued by the Army, they used load-bearing vests made locally and Vietnamese army packs. Instead of heavy air mattresses to sleep on, they carried hammocks that folded and rolled up so small they fit in a pocket-sized bag. Trying for every possible advantage, I did the same and equipped and prepared myself for survival in combat. Eventually, I used all of the common unauthorized equipment and more.

Anything to increase the odds of survival.

When I came home I almost died in a car wreck. I discovered a lot of returning veterans were getting killed in car wrecks. They had been away from driving for a year or more, so they had lost their touch. Many tended to drink a lot. They were at home where things were safe, so they relaxed to Condition White.

I quickly realized that driving, while not as dangerous as an infantry job in the combat zone, was dangerous, and I'd better develop the same no-nonsense attitude about it. "I will survive" applies to driving and the activities surrounding it.

2. Sound Tactics

Walking to your car in a dangerous mall parking lot requires tactics. Avoiding a red-light runner at an intersection requires tactics. Defeating a carjacker requires sound tactics. Just driving to work requires sound tactics. You do basic tactics unconsciously. The goal is so you do advanced tactics for virtually every situation unconsciously, and so you will follow sound tactics all of the time.

3. Competency with Your Weapon: Your Car

When my unit was static during the war, I practiced with my pistol and rifle incessantly. There were days my radio operator and I would use up a case of M-16 or a case of .45 ammunition in a day. The most dangerous weapon at my control, however, was a radio. With it I could call in artillery, helicopter gunships, and Air Force fighter-bombers. I studied all the ordnance at my command. I knew what each artillery piece would do, what the various helicopter weapons would do, and the types of various loads the Air Force fighter-bombers carried. When hit hard, I could quickly and effortlessly plan how to use the assets available. When I needed to use a weapon, whether it was the rifle or the radio, I didn't have to stop and think. I could operate on reflex and training.

With a car in today's traffic, it's no different. You should be able to use the phenomenal evasive characteristics of the modern automobile in a variety of ways without thinking, switching to instinct and training.

You Fight Like You Train

In combat, we were trained to react a certain way when we were ambushed. These were called immediate action drills. Every man would return fire instantly, full automatic. Turns were set up so that each man could empty a magazine at the enemy in full automatic mode without the entire unit having to reload at the same time. As each man fired up his magazine, he left the killing zone, covered by another man emptying his magazine. For 30 to 60 seconds the unit could put out enough firepower to keep the heads of the most determined enemy down. We practiced it until we got it right. Units that didn't practice it got cut to pieces in ambushes, and that happened a lot.

If you're trained in adequate tactics, you'll use them when you need to. For example, if you're taught proper braking techniques for anti-lock brake-equipped cars, you'll stop 100+ feet shorter from 60 mph than the average driver. That's one-third of a football field! If you're trained properly, you'll steer around obstacles when stopping isn't possible. If you're trained properly, you'll avoid carjackers' worst traps because you'll be alert, aware, and will do the little things that keep them from boxing you in.

Discipline

Only disciplined troops win wars. The North Vietnamese army was incredibly disciplined. They would crawl under barbed wire and attack a fire base with overwhelming firepower aimed at them.

It doesn't take as much discipline to drive to work, but it does take some. If you follow the advice in a later chapter and stay two seconds behind the car in front of you, in heavy traffic you will be constantly confronted with people pulling in front of you, filling up your safety zone with their car. The undisciplined driver either will try to retaliate by passing or tailgating the person who cut him off, or he will tailgate just to keep someone else from cutting in. All these responses are dangerous. The disciplined driver will sigh and drop back to two seconds behind the car who cut him off and ignore it and the next car who cuts him off. On my way to work this morning I was cut off four times. Three times a truck or car filled in the two-second space without using a signal. The fourth time a truck moved over without adequate clearance or a signal requiring me to brake heavily to preserve my bumper. Each time I had to fight the urge to retaliate. Each time it bugged me. But I have developed the discipline to let it go. The self-disciplined driver forces himself to ignore the idiots around him and concentrate on driving.

Accomplish the Mission

What's the mission of driving to work? It's not complicated. The mission of driving to work is to arrive on time without having any accidents. To do this you have to leave on time, and you have to concentrate on avoiding accidents. You can't expect anyone else to do it for you. In combat, accomplishing the mission is the highest priority. If in doubt, ask yourself when you strap yourself into the car, "What's my mission today?" "To get to work by 9 a.m." "To get the kids to daycare by 6:30 a.m." "To run errands." If you ever say, "to have an accident and kill myself," stop, take the keys, throw them on the roof, and stay home.

Keep the mission in mind. Accomplish it. Don't let anything keep you from it. Plan ahead for accomplishing each day's missions. If the mission next week will be to make it to work and back and your brakes are showing signs of wear, make an appointment to have them done. Don't leave home unprepared. Make sure you have a goal and that your car is fully up to the task.

No Excuses

Yes, Sir. No, Sir. No Excuse, Sir. Those are the first things a trainee learns in the military. Combat is serious business. People die. No excuses are asked for or accepted. Someone hit you while you were stopped at a traffic light. It was the other guy's fault. That's no excuse. Your car is still damaged. If it was a serious accident, you could still be dead.

The other guy ran a red light and hit you? No excuse. You should have avoided him. Your excuses might work to your boss, your spouse, your kids, or the police, but they won't work to you. You know you should have avoided the accident. They also won't work when you go to trade in the car if it was damaged in an accident. It's not worth as much as one that wasn't. The dealer will be able to tell. Not your fault? Too bad. The dealer or the next buyer doesn't care.

A commander is responsible for everything his men do or fail to do. Anything under your "command," such as your car, is your responsibility, period. If your car breaks down because you failed to get it maintained, it's your responsibility. If your passenger makes obscene gestures at a dangerous driver, provokes him, and he runs you off the road or shoots at you, it's your responsibility.

You are in the hospital, and the emergency room is working to save your life. "It wasn't my fault!" doesn't mean a thing to them. Right now it doesn't mean anything to you, either.

The Invisibility of Recon

The job of reconnaissance is not to fight the enemy but to find the enemy and return. Thus recon units go into harm's way and try to look invisible. Good ones succeed. Bad ones die. There's little in between. If you have a six-man Long Range Reconnaissance Patrol (LRRP, pronounced *lurp*), and you encounter an enemy battalion of 500 men, you'd better be invisible, because no matter how good you are, if he knows you're there, odds are you're not going home alive and kicking.

On the road there are recon drivers, and there are visible drivers. You need to be a recon driver and watch out for the visible ones. You'll see the visible drivers lurching around corners, exiting from the left lane, causing death and destruction wherever they go. A recon driver is a conservative, serious driver. You'll not see them on the road. You notice cars doing things wrong, correct? When you drove to work today, did you remember the van that turned left in front of you from the right lane, or the other 500 cars you interacted with that did nothing wrong? Being invisible just means going with the flow, not standing out, driving smoothly and unremarkably, watching everything that is going on that affects you.

Each troop in a recon unit is given an assigned sector to scan all of the time. You start on the left, scanning pie-shaped sections, near to far, then near on the next section to far, etc. When driving, scan in front of you, then the rearview mirror, then the side mirrors, then the front again. One of the reasons I like the left lane is you don't have to scan that mirror. A concrete wall can't move into you or cut you off.

Later chapters in this book will explain many special skills, such as evasive driving, the "stunts" like bootlegger hairpins, and cornering techniques, but these first two chapters are the key to survival. The combat mindset, situational awareness, the Color Code, discipline, and responsibility are your best weapons. Like most things in life, this is 90 percent mental. If you're trained well you have a better chance of survival. In the noncombat world the same is true. Study a few fatal accidents and you will see a pattern of behavior, actions that were indicative of poor training or discipline. How many fatalities that you hear about were people not wearing their seat belts? I kept track for a three-month period and didn't hear of any who *were* wearing their seat belts. This is basic stuff. Whether you're in a clapped-out Honda or a Mercedes S-Class, your odds of survival go up dramatically if you remember the combat mindset, situational awareness, discipline, and responsibility. And stay in Condition Yellow.

CHAPTER THREE

AVOIDING THE DUMB ACCIDENT

Most accidents are dumb. At least one of the participants had to do something dumb, and usually both did. This chapter is designed to make it less likely that the dumb one is you. It will also help you avoid other dumb drivers. This is basic stuff that you need before you can learn the advanced maneuvers. Before pilots can do eight-point hesitation rolls, they have to be able to take off and land.

The Mirror Trick

Do you feel you have a blind spot on each side of the car? Do you swivel your head a lot before changing lanes? When I was taking driver's education back in the dark ages, cars often had only a center mirror. A left fender mirror wasn't uncommon, but two outside mirrors were, and cars that had them often had no way of adjusting the mirror from inside the car, so they were always maladjusted. So we all learned to swivel our heads like fighter pilots if we wanted to change lanes without bashing fenders. Now virtually all cars have mirrors on both sides, however; and the one on the right is a convex mirror, so it'll cover a wide area. Unfortunately, most of us don't know how to use them. In fact, a large segment of drivers don't use them at all. Many people, when getting in a strange car, adjust the center mirror and perhaps the left outside mirror, ignoring the right mirror completely. They should have a bumper sticker required on anything they drive, "Caution—Driver may turn into you without warning!"

Take this book to your car and sit in the driver's seat. Look at the left mirror. Can you see the edge of your car?

Yes?

Now look at the right mirror. Can you see the edge of the car?

Yes?

Then *you're doing it wrong*. The center mirror is for looking behind you. The side mirrors are for covering your blind spots. You don't need three mirrors to see behind you. I talked to a recent graduate of driver education, and he told me he was being taught to adjust the mirrors until he could see the edge of the car. This tells me driver education is still doing it wrong. This doesn't surprise me. Have you asked any recent

Improper mirror alignment. If you can see the side of your car, your outside rearview mirror is adjusted too far in. A vehicle can hide outside your view.

Proper mirror alignment. Using the outside rearview mirror just for your blind spot, not for rear vision, means that a car will, as it moves out of the outside rearview mirror's view, come into your peripheral vision, eliminating blind spots.

The trick mirror. The little Brookstone mirror, mounted in your left outside rearview mirror, will cover the blind spot for tall drivers who can't move the factory mirror far out enough.

Top: Mirrors, Incorrect

Driver doesn't see either car in either blind spot, but he sees three images of what's behind him.

Improper mirror alignment. If you can see the side of your car, your outside rearview mirror is adjusted too far in. A vehicle can hide outside your view.

Bottom: Mirrors, Correct

Both blind spots are covered.

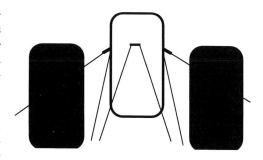

high school graduate any questions lately, like "What countries border the United States?" or "What countries were we fighting during World War II?" They don't know that, either.

Here's how to do it right.

Sitting in the driver's seat, lean over until your head touches the side window glass. Now adjust the mirror out until you can just see the edge of the car—with your head touching the side window glass.

Now lean over until you're in the middle of the car. Adjust the right mirror out until you can just see the edge of the car—with your head in the middle of the car.

Now sit in your normal position. The center mirror should show you who is behind you. The left mirror should show you who is in your left blind spot. The right mirror should show you who is in your right blind spot.

I should note that I do not take credit for discovering this particular method of adjusting the mirrors. I did, however, learn to adjust my mirrors farther out than the lamented driver's education instructor had told me. I discovered my mirrors were too far in by near accident—literally! I changed lanes and discovered a Ford in my target spot.

"I don't get it," I thought. "I looked in my mirror." So I drove up next to a car and pulled forward until he was in my left blind spot. Then I adjusted the mirror out until I could see him. I did the same thing for the right side. Since then I've always adjusted the mirrors out. Then I began to see other people recommending it. Bill Buff, in his driving school, Driving Dynamics, recommended it. The National Motorists Association recommended it. Denise McCluggage, in her electronic publication, *roadrunning.com*, recommended it. And *Radar Reporter* described how to adjust the mirrors as I've described. Since then I've been trying to teach it.

The Trick Mirror

Sometimes, in some cars, adjusting the mirrors all the way out isn't enough. My seating position is such that I must adjust most mirrors all the way out. The right mirror, with its *"Objects May Be Closer Than They Appear"'* warning, is convex, so it covers the blind spot adequately. The left mirror, using flat glass by federal edict, doesn't cover the blind spot on some cars. I've developed the habit of swiveling my head often or just moving it to the right until I can see the blind spot in the mirror.

While in the store one day I discovered a small rectangular stick-on mirror with a matte black plastic frame, almost matching the mirrors on my car, designed to fit on the lower inside edge of the left mirror and angled out properly to catch the blind spot. It looked better than the round ones you see on trucks, and when I installed it, it worked like a charm. If it didn't have the store's name on it, it would almost look as if the folks at the factory intended it to go there.

The Two-Second Rule

In some states, if you get a speeding ticket, you're forced to take one of those godawful defensive driving courses. One of the things they're teaching right is the two-second rule. When I took driver's ed. back in the Mesozoic age, they taught us how many car lengths to be behind the car ahead at what speed. It was complicated, and most drivers never figured out how to judge how long a car was anyway. I always wondered, what kind of car? Is it a Cadillac stretch limo, or is it an Austin-Healey Sprite?

The two-second rule works. Simply watch the car ahead pass some fixed object, and count "One thousand one, one thousand two." You should cross the object at about "two" (longer in bad weather, of course).

This is simple, effective, and easy to remember. The following two things will happen:

1. You will be very unlikely to hit the car ahead of you. This is especially important in states like Texas, where the guy behind is always at fault, even if the guy ahead is his accomplice in an insurance-fraud scheme, which has become a major scam industry in the state.

2. Countless cars will cut you off, pulling in front of you without signaling. For some reason, most of them will immediately slow down. This is a test of maturity. If you have the maturity of a saint, you will ignore them and drop back to give them two seconds. If you whip around them and slam on your brakes, collecting their car into your back seat, you failed the maturity test.

Avoiding the "Crossing the Median" Fender Bender

Actually, this isn't always a merely fender bender. I saw a fatality happen because of this. If you're crossing a median and stopped in the middle, whether you're turning left or U-turning, most people do a couple of things wrong. They stop with the tail of their car sticking out in the lane when the median is wide enough to take the whole car, thus protecting it from traffic. And they forget they're driving on the right and move to the left, like so:

U-Turn/Crossing the Median, Incorrect
White car is blocking the car behind him, and if a car comes to turn from the other direction, he is blocked, too. The likelihood of the white car causing an accident is quite high. Either he will be hit by a car coming up behind him, or someone will change lanes to avoid him. Gray car, blocked by white car, just stops, blocking vision of white car. At this point gray car should probably just go ahead and turn short like the white car. But if it does, then both of them have blocked vision.

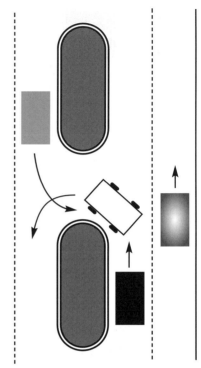

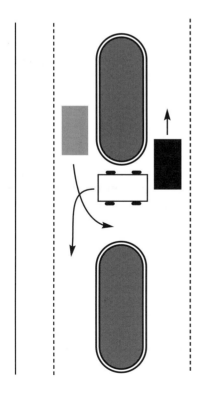

U-turn
White car is on right side of U-turn. Gray car, still being driven by an idiot, stops, blocking his left lane and blocks vision of white car. If you're the white car, there's nothing you can do but wave him on. At least you won't get the rear end clipped.

26

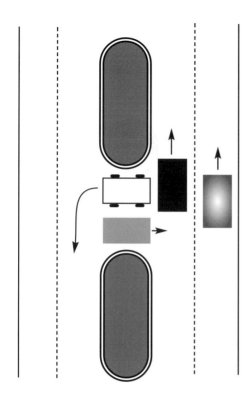

U-turn, Correct
White car is on right side of U-turn. Gray car is on the right side of the U-turn. His IQ just went up 50 points. Both can see oncoming traffic, neither is in danger of being hit.

How to Maximize Anti-lock Brakes

The average person does not understand anti-lock brakes (ABS). Antilock Brakes might be the biggest active safety invention of the latter half of the twentieth century. Sadly, they are misused and misunderstood enough to make them far less effective than they should be.

Antilock Braking Systems, invented by Mercedes-Benz in 1954, have become highly sophisticated. A computer reads wheel lockup on each wheel (or each axle on some solid-axle cars), and releases brake pressure for a split second to unlock the brakes, then reapplies brake pressure. Anti-lock systems act as normal brakes until the point of lockup has been exceeded, then the pumping action is felt and heard by the driver. The pedal will kick back and vibrate or pulsate, and the pumping noise will be heard. If the first time you've ever heard this noise and felt this pulsating is in an emergency, you might assume something is wrong with the brakes and take your foot off and start pumping them—as several police officers did with early ABS-equipped police Chevrolet Caprices. This is a mistake, and with some of the police officers involved, it was a fatal mistake.

ABS Practice Exercises

Before there is an emergency, drive your car to a deserted road, at least deserted enough that you can do a few hard stops. Check the rearview mirror to make sure you're alone, accelerate to 30 mph, and stand on the brake pedal. Listen for the noise. Note the feel of the pedal. Keep your foot on the pedal until the car stops. Now try it again, with a little less pressure. Instead of *pulse-pulse-pulse-pulse*, you'll note *pulse . . . pulse . . . pulse*. Now do it again until you can modulate the brakes enough that you feel that pulse about once a second. This is threshold braking. This will give you the shortest stopping distances because the brakes are at optimum, right at the threshold of lockup. The pumping of ABS brakes will actually lengthen stopping distances slightly beyond this. (In a panic, it's best to stand on the brakes too hard and let them do the modulating than it is to be too easy on them and fail to stop in time.)

If you cannot train yourself to use threshold braking in an emergency, it's better to use full ABS and worry about steering gently around the problem if possible, which brings us to the second exercise. On a deserted road, to do a panic full ABS-stop and very gently change lanes one lane left, then back again, simulating the situation shown here. Practice this procedure very carefully, preferably in an area that won't hurt you if you spin, like a big parking lot without curbs. (Of course, the parking lot security guard won't understand.)

Extra braking problems come when it's wet or snowy, or when you can't quite get the threshold down. Some cars are very sensitive. Others can be held on the threshold quite easily. Go past the threshold, and on non-ABS-equipped cars something locks up. If it's the front wheels, you'll slide in a straight line. If it's the rear brakes, the rear will come around, and, unless you release the brakes and counter steer, you'll spin. If it's one front or one rear brake, then things become difficult. The car will jerk in one direction or another or become directionally unstable. For example, many pre-'94 Mustangs will lock up the right front tire first. The best solution is ABS brakes.

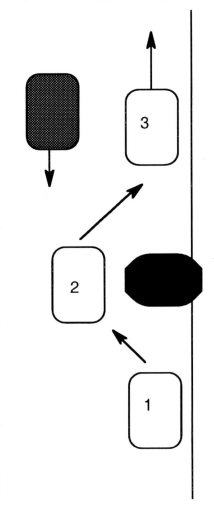

This is the proverbial "car pulled out of nowhere." It is stopped within your stopping distance, so you must evade, but a car is oncoming, so you must be back in your lane ASAP.

Insurance companies say anti-lock brakes don't lower accident rates. What they've decided is that accidents involving ABS cars hitting other cars go down, and accidents involving non-ABS cars hitting ABS cars go up. Non-ABS cars following ABS cars don't have the control and pile into ABS cars. Additionally, one-car accidents go up. Many drivers successfully avoid something in their way, and in the process lose control of their cars and smash into something else all by themselves.

Why?

Let's back up and make sure we understand some basic principles—specifically, a locked wheel does not steer. You've probably learned this the hard way. If you've ever stood on the brakes of a non-ABS car in panic and then tried to turn to avoid the obstacle that's the source of the panic, well, as you slid into the problem, you might have well said, "Eureka! A locked wheel does not steer!" Your car is just like a brick sliding down the road, and bricks don't steer. That's why bricks don't have steering wheels.

Locked wheels also scrub off rubber from the patch of tire surface sliding down the road. The result is a flat-spotted tire. Flat spot a tire and you'll have to replace it or put up with an awful vibration. If a racing driver flat spots a tire he has to make a pit stop. At high speeds, the vibration will tear the car apart or cause it to crash from the loss in stability.

Because of this, many people were taught to stay off the brakes during emergencies. In certain situations that technique is justified. At the accident avoidance simulator at the Bob Bondurant School of High Performance Driving, you drive down the middle lane of a "road" bounded by pylons. The road widens to three lanes, each with its own traffic light. At the last second two of them, including your middle lane, turn red, and you must go for the green lane. If you slam on the brakes, you won't make the turn. You'll transfer the vehicle's weight forward, loading up the front wheels and unloading the rears. If the brakes are locked, you won't turn, and you'll run the red light in the middle lane. If the brakes aren't locked up, the tail (now unloaded) will come around as the front wheels (heavily loaded) will really turn the front. So you'll have a lurid, cone-filled spin, and Mr. Bondurant will teach you a lesson you will never forget.

What many people do is stand on the brakes, then jerk the steering wheel and unload the brakes, causing the car to slow drastically, and then turn while the wheels are unlocked.

But with ABS brakes, if you jerk the wheel, the car will turn even more effectively while braking than it will under normal circumstances. When braking hard, the ABS brakes are at near optimum, just below lockup. The weight transfer is already complete, with most of the weight riding on the front tires. Seventy-five percent of the braking is done by the front wheels of an ABS car, and only 25 percent is done by

A Valentine Research G-Analyst. This relatively inexpensive device can be mounted in any vehicle to record G-forces in acceleration, braking, and cornering. It is a useful performance-measuring, and thus performance-enhancing, tool.

the rear brakes. This makes your steering hypereffective under heavy braking. Yank the front wheel in a panic turn and you will lose control of the car. This is when the one-car accidents occur. The novice ABS driver avoids the problem in a panic but winds up in a field wondering why and how he got there. You must steer gently, and smoothly. Steer, figuratively, with your fingertips. Give steering inputs at 80 to 90 percent of what you think you'll need. Don't overdo it.

So the proper thing to do is to brake hard, hard enough to activate the ABS (ideally just barely for threshold braking). On a racetrack I would want to hear the ABS pumping maybe once or twice a second, then I would know I was braking hard enough. In a panic situation you might hear it pumping 14 to 30 times a second. If you can feather the brakes just a bit, you'll stop shorter, but under adrenaline, fear, and stress, do the best you can. Stress driving isn't 100 percent, it's the best you can do under the circumstances. Success is measured in an on/off manner. If you avoid the accident, you win. You did it right. If you didn't—well, then you did it wrong, and you need more practice.

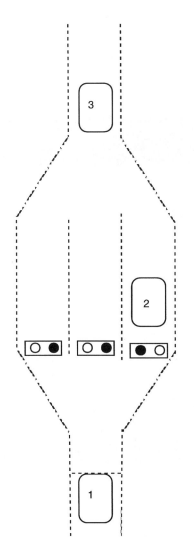

Bondurant Accident Avoidance Simulator
Position 1: Car approaching at 30–40 mph crosses pneumatic sensor. Two green lights turn red, one turns green, indicating one clear lane with the other two blocked. Lacking ABS brakes, the driver should not brake, but accelerate slightly to transfer weight to rear, and steer into green light lane at position 2.

Position 3. Driver must steer back into center lane. Test, as set up, is easy at 30 mph, difficult at 40 mph.

Incident 2

I was driving down a four-lane undivided suburban road with a companion in the passenger's seat. It had just started to rain. The road was very slippery because fresh rain brings oils in the road to the surface. A car ahead went to the left turn lane and braked. The tail came around and he spun, blocking our lane. I braked hard, hearing the ABS going thud-thud-thud . . . thud . . . thud *as I feathered them. Very gently I steered around him, as I would a wreck on a racetrack. I made a point to turn the wheel just a little less than seemed necessary. It's smoother, and smooth is fast. It also avoids loss of control due to overcontrol.*

Cutting Emergency Stopping Distances in Half

The other misuse of ABS brakes is not to use them hard enough, soon enough. This so bugged the engineers at Mercedes-Benz that they invented Brake Assist™, which reads the speed at which you go from throttle to brake and applies full ABS braking as soon as you touch the pedal in an emergency—and only in an emergency. Assuming you don't have a new Mercedes, try doing this yourself.

For the purpose of this exercise, let's assign numbers to braking effort. 0 is no braking, 1 is light, 9 is full ABS. We discovered most novice racing students at Porsche Club schools would approach a corner braking like this:

0—1—1—1—2—2—2—3—3—4—5—6—7—8—9—9—9—9—0

On a G-Meter, the graph of braking forces would look like this, with the vertical axis being Gs, the horizontal axis being time:

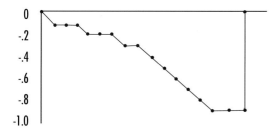

In other words, the more they slowed, the more they braked. They did most of their hardest braking at the slower speeds. But at the higher speeds is when braking is most important. At 60 mph you're moving 88 feet per second. Additionally, going from 9 on braking into a hard corner was difficult, and spins occurred. The result of this braking technique was longer braking distances, slower lap times, and more spins and fouled-up corners. A second of hard braking at 60 is much more effective than one at 30 mph.

So we taught this style:

0-3-5-7-9—9—9—9—9—9—9—9—9-8-7-6-5-4-3-2-1-0

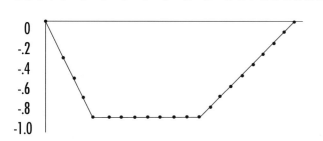

The result was much shorter stopping distances, later braking points on the track, faster cornering because of the smoother transition, thus shorter lap times. If you can delay braking on a race track, obviously your lap times will go down. You are going fastest just before the brakes are applied. Delaying braking 0.10 second at 120 mph means you will spend that 0.10 second going 176 feet per second. The man who brakes 0.10 second later than you will be a car length ahead of you at the other end of the track. Back when Ayrton Senna was driving for the McLaren F1 team, the telemetry showed that the difference between him and their test driver was that Senna braked 0.10 second later at virtually every corner.

On the street it means you will stop in 40 percent shorter time than the person who hesitates his way into the brakes. Forty percent! In Mercedes tests, volunteers averaged 239 feet stopping from 100 km/hr (62 mph). Using the brakes properly, the car stopped in 131 feet.

If you get good at stopping quickly, be sure to watch your rearview mirrors. The person behind you might not know this technique. Remember, since you're already driving in Condition Yellow, which you learned in the first chapter, you will know whether someone is close behind you because you will have checked your mirrors a few seconds ago.

Steering Around Accidents

Back when I suggested two ABS exercises, I had an ulterior motive. The second exercise, steering around the car that had pulled out in front of you while trying to stop, demonstrated what to do when things happen within your stopping distance. If you're going 60 mph, and something happens within 130 feet of you, the best racing driver in the best car is going to be hard pressed to miss it. Perfect brakes, perfect tires, a high traction, clean braking surface, and perfect reflexes will get you a low-speed collision unless you steer around the obstacle. The best cars can stop in 130 feet, but add even .25 seconds for reflexes (and that's good), and you'll need 22 feet more. If something happens 50 feet in front of you, steering around it is the only option, so you must be prepared to do so. This sounds pretty basic, but the average driver, confronted with a block of concrete 50 feet in front of his car, will stand on the brakes and hit it centered, with no effort to steer around it.

The Bob Bondurant School of High Performance Driving's Accident Avoidance Simulator trains drivers to handle this nicely and justifies taking the course just for that simulator. It's a fixture of all of his basic courses.

Using Situational Awareness

How often do you check your rearview mirror? Remember the game we played in Chapter One? Every time someone surprises you in your rearview mirror, give yourself some penance. You should *always, always, always* know who is in your rear-view mirror, and who is on either side of you. If the car ahead of you drops a proverbial smoking bomb out of the trunk, which way can you dodge? Is there a car in your left blind spot? Your right? O.K., there's a car on each side, but you've got to dodge the smoking bomb? Which car is bigger? You should know these things. If one is a Miata, you can punt him out of the way to avoid something more dangerous. (Sorry, Miata drivers.) If it's a Suburban, it's more difficult, but we'll show you how in a later chapter.

Constantly scan the area around you. Scan ahead from near to far, scan the rearview mirror, then the side mirrors, then the gauges, then down the road from near to far, then the rearview mirror, then the side mirrors. In heavy traffic, do it more often than while alone on an empty freeway, of course.

Don't forget the gauges. Running out of fuel gets you a lot of demerits. Overheating an engine gets you even more.

The Two-Second Pause at Green Lights

Intersection crashes are getting more and more common as well as more and more deadly. Running red lights has become so much of a sport that an auto parts store made up bumper stickers saying, "I brake for red lights." They stopped giving them out when it was determined that no one knew what they were talking about.

Basic defensive driving means you stop when the light turns yellow if you can without locking up the brakes. Advanced defensive driving means when you're stopped for a red light and it turns green, you count "One thousand one, one thousand two," and then go, swiveling your head both ways before going when the light turns green. A basic rule is the person running the light 1.5 seconds late is going flat out. He isn't creeping through the intersection. If he hits you, you will know it. If he hits you in the driver's door, the crumple zone is small to nonexistent. Most cars aren't designed to take side impacts well. He'll walk away. You probably won't. Current cars are built to withstand a 30 mph side impact. Most do quite poorly at 35 mph. At 40 mph or more the car brands that are built strong enough for you to survive can be counted on one hand. One in three fatalities is from a side impact. Most of the time someone ran a red light, pure and simple.

Right on Red, Stop First

Another very bad habit some people have is to fly through a right-on-red situation. If you're the person going through the green light, expect at least one person to do a flying right on red. This means going through the intersection at a speed and in a manner that will enable you to avoid him. Going through the intersection with your foot poised over the brake is not unreasonable. Additionally, try to have a "steer around" plan in mind (though right-on-red runners often turn into the middle or left lane, making avoidance even more tricky).

34

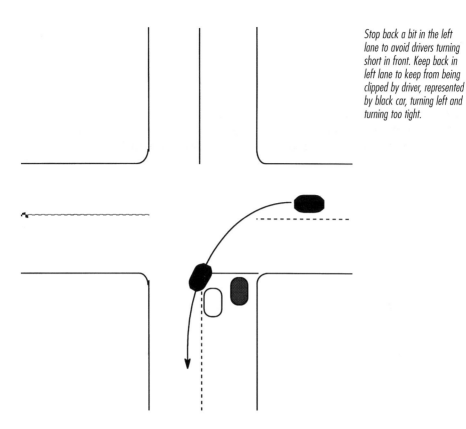

Stop back a bit in the left lane to avoid drivers turning short in front. Keep back in left lane to keep from being clipped by driver, represented by black car, turning left and turning too tight.

Intimidation Driving

Needless to say, this is a no-no. Tailgating smaller vehicles, driving in blind spots, dirty looks, and impatient gestures make some people move over, but more often than not, the person being intimidated decides they've had enough. Some people will even go as far as to wait until you glance away, haul back on their hand brake, and then stand on the brakes, effectively causing a rear-end collision. It'll be your fault, your insurance rate increases, and your ticket. The other driver can collect against your insurance for whiplash and pain and suffering.

Things You Don't Do in Your Own Nest

I'm constantly amazed at the bad driving habits exhibited by people within sight of their own garages. Soon all of your neighbors know you're a jerk. The likelihood you will be confronted by either a large, angry neighbor or a committee of the same is high, and retaliation by neighbors who don't like being run off the road or fearing for their children on bicycles in close proximity to someone who drives 50 in a school zone is quite high. Even if you drive like a total maniac, measure a couple of miles from your house and declare a truce there. Most accidents happen within five miles of home at speeds below 25 miles an hour anyway. The cure isn't, despite what the joke says, to always drive 40 and never go home. The cure is to treat the area around home as a danger zone and drive accordingly.

Light Usage

For some reason it seems the drivers of silver cars are the last to turn on their headlights, and they're the most invisible. Perhaps they want to be invisible. Your lights should be on in any sort of inclement weather, well before dusk and after dawn, and any time your wipers are on. Daytime running lights (DRLs) ensure your headlights are on all the time. This is not necessarily good. NHTSA-funded studies have shown no lower accident rates using DRLs. The additional glare could be causing accidents, and some DRLs have a fatal flaw: The taillights don't come on with them. So the driver, seeing his headlights on, thinks he has taillights at night. Ideally DRLs, if used, should be set up like those on Volvos. The dash lights don't come on with the DRLs. The fog lights won't work with them, either. You must turn on your headlights to get those. Additionally, the taillights do come on with the DRLs (a useless feature in the daytime, but a good safety feature for those who forget to switch over to the real things at night).

Aim High

Back when I was taking that driver's ed. course, my school used a filmed presentation of the Smith System, a simple system proven to lower accident rates among fleets. The teenagers giggled or slept through it, of course. The only thing I can remember of it is "Aim high in driving." It's still excellent advice.

When cornering on a racetrack, as a racing driver brakes for a turn, his eyes are on the apex, the point of the corner where his inside wheels come closest to the inside edge of the track. As he reaches the apex, his eyes are at the exit. After a few laps, he's looking even farther, the entrance to the next corner as he enters the first. The late Ayrton Senna admitted he was looking and planning one, sometimes two corners ahead while he drove. The same thing works on the road. Stare at the brake lights ahead of you, and sooner or later you'll have a stupid accident. You should be looking as far ahead as possible. This is one reason why trucks and SUVs are so popular in the United States. They sit up high, with a "command" driving position, enabling their drivers to see over other traffic. (Except, of course, now that all of the other traffic is SUVs and pickup trucks, no one can see over anyone else and we're back to square one.)

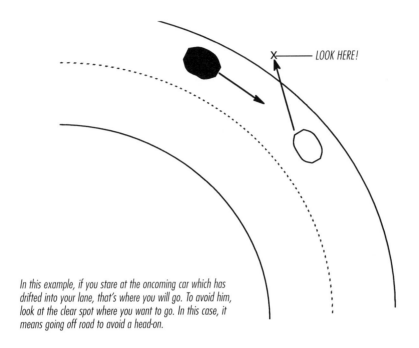

LOOK HERE!

In this example, if you stare at the oncoming car which has drifted into your lane, that's where you will go. To avoid him, look at the clear spot where you want to go. In this case, it means going off road to avoid a head-on.

Look Where You Want to Go

Just as in firing a gun you shoot at what you're looking at, your car will go where you're looking. If you're trying to avoid a car, don't look at the car but at the spot you're trying to get to.

Machismo Control

Driving can be very stressful. Someone cuts you off, and you find a way to get ahead of them and pay them back. Occasionally another driver will try something really stupid like passing you on the shoulder, and it really makes you angry. The result is a lot of stressful drivers with an enraged bad driver now trying to get even with you. The bad driver has already proven he's an idiot. Let him go. You don't want to be around him when he self-destructs, lest he take you with him.

This is tough for everyone. While this book is subtitled *Combat Survival Techniques for the Road*, one combat analogy too many does not work. You are not in combat. If someone intrudes on your territory, you do not retaliate. When my unit was in Vietnam, if we found North Vietnamese army troops near us, we would try to kill them. This is not applicable on the road. Remember the recon analogy. If you consider every jerk driver to be a greatly superior enemy force, you will not pick a fight with him just because he cut you off. You will stay out of his way and stay invisible.

Stupid Things You Can Do at Railroad Tracks

All accidents involving trains are stupid, dumb accidents. Unfortunately, they're nearly all fatal to the car's occupants. They are also always the car driver's fault. Most of them occur at tracks that the drivers encounter often. So they can't say they didn't know the tracks were there. Even if all the signs are missing it's hard to camouflage railroad tracks.

The cure? Simple. Always stop behind the signal arms. If the signal arms go down while you're waiting, no problem. Stop on the tracks, problem. A large number of accidents involve drivers who go *around* the barricades. While waiting for a train to pass I've had people pass me while I was stopped just behind the white line. One had a signal arm lower on his roof. Another had to back up to avoid the train. All I could do was shake my head.

If someone has done something stupid around you and is going to be hit by the train, be aware that you're in danger. The collision will be quite violent, and flying debris will be dangerous. Leaving your car to avoid the damage is a reasonable strategy. Run in the opposite direction of the train's travel. If, for example, the train is going west, go east.

Needless to say, if the guy in front of you stops too close to the tracks, leave room behind him. He might be backing up.

The Cellular Phone: A Fantastic, Extremely Useful Tool That Kills People

Studies have shown that drivers using cellular phones are as dangerous as drunk drivers. Hands-free phones should help, but apparently they don't. This doesn't mean you shouldn't use the hands-free feature. Not only that, you should practice answering the phone without looking at it. You should be able to find the "Send" button by feel. Of course, outgoing calls should be started only when you're stopped. Having preset memories that you can access by feel or by voice activation helps. And 911 should be accessible by feel, either by pushing and holding "1," as on Motorola phones, or by voice activation.

Seat Belts, Seat Belts, Seat Belts

Not having the seat belt fastened makes a minor incident into a major accident. When I was a child, a neighbor had a little fender bender half a block from her house. Unfortunately, her child, unrestrained in the front seat, hit the dash at 12 mph and was killed. An adult's head in a 12-mph impact will go halfway through the windshield. So even the trip to the store at the end of the block requires a seat belt, and a child safety seat for a child under 12 years old or 100 pounds. Do not belt the child in the same seat belt with the parent. Even in a mild collision, the child will be crushed.

Bad Weather Modifications to Your Driving

An amazing number of people drive the same in the rain as they do when it's dry. This is as bad as a driver who constantly drives 50 mph no matter what the speed limit. The best drivers show the most variations in speed due to conditions. On a bright, dry, windless day, make hay while the sun shines. When it's raining and visibility is 200 feet, it's time to tread gently and drive carefully. Passing vehicles that cause large amounts of road spray, such as 18-wheelers, requires extra caution.

CHAPTER FOUR

High-Performance Driving Techniques for the Road

Nineteen eighty-one—I was driving up the Gulf Freeway, I-45, in Houston, Texas, to work when somehow a pickup truck came off the overpass above me, going the wrong way, down the grass, spinning and rolling, coming to stop in the middle lane of I-45, one or two car lengths in front of me. Reflexively, I turned the steering wheel, changing lanes violently, scraping past the wreckage, and then, still on reflexes, returning to my lane. Then the adrenaline shock hit, and I drove slowly in the right lane until I could pull off and park for a minute. Another car driving behind me had hit the pickup, without braking, at 60 to 70 mph. I couldn't get back to the scene of the accident, but I learned later fatalities resulted. Had I hit the pickup at 60 mph in the vehicle I was driving, I'm sure that one of the fatalities would have been me.

Incidents like this are why you need to know high-performance driving techniques. Not for everyday driving—which more and more consists of watching the brake lights of the car creeping along in front of you until it's your exit—but for emergencies. When the truck falls out of the sky in front of you, landing one car length in front of you on the freeway, you need to know violent evasive maneuvers, and what to do when the car gets sideways.

Once upon a time I was a young lieutenant stationed in Great Britain at an Air Force base. How a young Army lieutenant gets stationed at an Air Force base is another story, but at the time an intelligence officer and I were into racing, and it came to the attention of the wing safety officer. He called us into his office and said he had a problem. He was losing highly trained officers and airmen at an alarming rate on the British roads. He surmised that a lot of the young men were buying sports cars and racing on public roads. He was willing to sponsor a club to allow them to race on unused runways to get it out of their systems safely. We asked for the accident reports to study. After a couple of days we reported back that what they needed was not a place to race, but training.

A lot of the accidents were one-car accidents, often in high-performance cars. And the accident reports indicated they were getting in over their heads and not knowing how to get out of the situation. One involved a Lotus Elan, a very high-strung sports car. The driver was mystified as to how it happened. He had downshifted as he pulled out to pass another car and wound up in the ditch. We figured out pretty quickly that jerking the wheel while downshifting roughly had caused the rear wheels to lose adhesion, and the car went into a rear wheel skid, ending in a ditch.

So we suggested advanced training. The wing got British police instructors to set up the school, blocked off some runway access roads, got the fire trucks to flood the course for the skid school, and taught the personnel how to stay alive. If you owned or bought what the base considered a high-performance car, you were required to take the training, and if you had a car not so designated, you could still take the training. The training included skid control and accident avoidance.

The Air Force is not a democracy but a dictatorship, and thus the Base Commander could require people to get the training.

Sit, Fido, Sit

And the first thing you need to know is how to sit.

(Oh, come on, Rich. I've been sitting behind a wheel since I was thirteen.)

Oh, really? I sit in cars with hundreds of people each year, and most of them don't know how to sit. If you do, humor me. Read this section anyway.

First, obviously, you need to be able to reach the pedals comfortably. Adjust the seat until you can, where you can completely depress the clutch, if there is one, where your left foot can rest comfortably on the dead pedal.

What's a dead pedal? Will it smell up my car?

The dead pedal is a place to rest your left foot when it's not in use on the clutch. With an automatic transmission it's even more important. Your feet should be so placed that your left foot can brace against the dead pedal. Really good driver's cars all have dead pedals. If your car doesn't, you probably should *get rid of it.*

Now, adjust the seat back until you're comfortable. With your back touching the seatback, place one hand over the steering wheel, arm fully extended. Ideally, your wrist should be touching the steering wheel. If your fingers barely touch it, you're too far away; and if, with your arm straight, your forearm is touching the wheel, you're too close.

With your fingers barely touching, you'll be unable to use your shoulders in violent evasive maneuvers, and you'll unconsciously be pulling yourself up out of the seatback in order to control the car. This costs you the loss of the seatback's lateral support, and it becomes tiring.

A lot of middle-aged enthusiast guys tend to drive this way because when we were growing up in the late fifties and sixties the Grand Prix drivers were lying down on the job. But they were doing it because of the design of the cars. In an effort to get the cars' frontal area down, the drivers were reclined to a pretty much lying-down position. Additionally, GP cars might have one turn lock to lock, so a driver could, by crossing his arms, go to full lock without taking his hands off the wheel. You can't do that on your family sedan with four turns lock to lock.

Women, on the other hand, tend to sit too close to the steering wheel. In that position they're unable to move the steering wheel far enough in an evasive situation without their elbows hitting various parts of their anatomy. Additionally, on air bag–equipped cars, they're sitting too close to the air bag.

An air bag must inflate in approximately 1/30 second. To do so it leaves its holder at 200 mph. At the time of writing, lower powered air bags are still a future item due to Federal law. Air bags are designed, by law, to be able to restrain a 200-pound driver, unbelted, in a 30-mph barrier crash test. This leaves air bags with excess power for small drivers who are belted in and sitting too close to the wheel—in low-speed collisions. Your driving position should give you 10 inches minimum between the air bag and your chest. If it doesn't, you should readjust it.

If some people still refuse to cooperate, I give up. This is something you have to do yourself. Either you will, or you won't. People still smoke, drink to excess, and eat fatty meats, and no amount of preaching will convert them. So I don't preach the gospel of proper seating position.

Hand Position on the Steering Wheel

The Bob Bondurant School of High Performance Driving and the other racing and high-performance driving schools teach the 9 and 3 o'clock driving position, meaning mentally put a clock face on the steering wheel with 12 o'clock being straight up. Your left hand should be at 9 o'clock, and your right hand should be at 3 o'clock. The 10 and 2 o'clock position was taught to many of us in driver's ed., and a considerable number of drivers will swear by it. At least one Grand Prix driver uses it, and he drives a lot faster and makes a lot more money doing it than I do, so I won't argue with him. It has some disadvantages, however, especially with air bag-equipped cars. In a crash you really want your arms to be out of the way of the air bag. According to a friend at an emergency room, broken arms due to air bags do show up in emergency rooms now and then. But at the 9 and 3 position your arms are out of the way.

Traditionally, you hooked your thumbs over the spokes at that position except for those two-spoked steering wheels American car manufacturers have started using, usually with thumb rests on the inside of the wheel at 9 and 3. They're at least providing those some of the time. When they don't, there's less to hang the thumbs on. The purpose of hanging your thumbs is so the wheel won't be wrenched out of your hand when a front tire catastrophically blows. However, as suspension geometry improves this isn't as much of a problem with many cars as it was in the old days. If a tire blows in a lot of high quality late model cars, the car isn't likely to yank one way or another.

What *does* happen with the thumbs locked over the spokes is broken thumbs if you slide into a wall. Hence if you're driving an open-wheel race car on a racetrack, you adopt the thumbs up driving position, with your thumbs pointed up. This works well if you're passing the wheel through your hands on a street vehicle, too.

It also is preferable if you have an air bag-equipped car.

Passing the Wheel vs. Hand-Over-Hand

When I took driver's ed., they taught the hand-over-hand method to cope with five-turn lock-to-lock nonpower steering, and I used it until I was stationed in England. American military personnel in England didn't have to get British driver's licenses, but we were trained in British regulations and techniques. Dependents were required to get British driver's licenses after two years, and the bureaucracy of the British system was such that it usually took them two years if they started taking driver's tests when they arrived. The British testers would fail them for using hand-over-hand techniques. When I learned that I started trying their method of passing the wheel through your hands. It *is* superior. You don't get crossed up, which is a real problem with air bag–equipped cars, and you have better control. The secret of going fast is smoothness and precise control. (You will be reading this again.)

To make a left turn by passing the wheel through your hands, for example, move your left hand from 9 o'clock to 12 o'clock and push up with your right hand. Now both hands are touching at the 12 o'clock position. Pull your left hand down, taking the steering wheel with it, simultaneously moving your right hand to the 6 o'clock position. Now both hands are touching at 6 o'clock. Now push up with your right hand and move your left hand up. Obviously, depending on the tightness of the turn, you may only have to do this once, and ideally you'll wind up with your hands at 9 and 3 for the main part of the turn. The hands never cross, and you always have a pretty good idea where center is for the steering wheel.

A surprising number of people turn the wheel with their hands inside it, as in the middle photo on page 46. I don't know where they got it, and I don't know why they do it. Perhaps they feel they can exert more force, upper body strength once being a problem in driving in the days before power steering. There's nothing to say about it except that it's a bad habit.

Sitting too close to the steering wheel, this driver can't move the wheel far enough for a violent evasive maneuver. Additionally, she is too close to the air bag. A 10-inch minimum clearance is needed for survival.

Sitting too far from the steering wheel, this driver can't use her shoulders for violent evasive maneuvers. This was a popular style in the '60s because Grand Prix drivers seemed to drive this way. But due to the design of the cars, they had to. Plus, they weren't coping with three to four turns lock to lock.

After adjusting the seat so that your feet comfortably touch the pedals, put one arm out straight while still touching the seatback. Your wrist should reach the top of the wheel. If you have to use your hand to reach the wheel, you're too far away. If your wrist overlaps, you're too close. This driver is the proper distance from the wheel both with hands and feet to control the car. This is a safe distance from the air bag, too.

Wrong steering-wheel hand position: Hands are too high on the wheel for full control in emergencies. Also, arms will be hit by air bag in a crash.

Correct steering-wheel hand position for non-air bag–equipped steering wheel: 9 o'clock and 3 o'clock. Before air bags, hooking the thumbs over the steering wheel was a good idea.

Correct steering-wheel hand position for air bag–equipped steering wheel. Thumbs are up (hence the "Thumbs Up" driving position), fingers wrapped around wheel. Danger from air bag is minimized. This also works for open-wheeled race cars. When you hit the wall, you won't break your thumbs.

Wrong: Hand-over-hand steering is wrong for a lot of reasons. It leaves you crossed up at times and with only one hand on the wheel, and in a crash those arms will be hit by the air bag.

Wrong. No one ever taught this in driver's ed., but I see it daily, usually by women drivers: hand inside the steering wheel. There is both danger of air bag deployment and it's difficult to control the car.

Correct: Pass the wheel through the hands. This gives you the sensitivity to know what's going on between the rubber and the road. Both hands are always on the wheel, and they're out of the way of an air bag. When making a left turn, first move the left hand to 12 o'clock . . .

Push the wheel up with the right hand, with the hands meeting in this slight exaggeration. Then pull the left hand down and slide the right hand down . . .

. . . which puts the hands at 9 and 3 for a lot of corners. This, on a long sweeper, for example, leaves the arms in the strongest position, and gives good sensitivity. In a tighter turn, continue sliding the hands through the wheel . . .

. . . where the hands, in this slight exaggeration, meet. I don't find my hands meeting in actual driving, but I might in parking. My student in this photo said it felt unnatural, but after a couple of days she was used to it. I've been doing it since 1969, and it has become so instinctive that I have to watch myself doing it in order to figure it out to explain it to students.

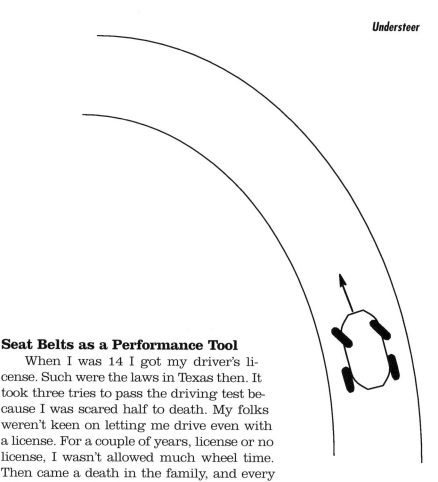

Seat Belts as a Performance Tool

When I was 14 I got my driver's license. Such were the laws in Texas then. It took three tries to pass the driving test because I was scared half to death. My folks weren't keen on letting me drive even with a license. For a couple of years, license or no license, I wasn't allowed much wheel time. Then came a death in the family, and every driver was needed for the activities surrounding the funeral, and I started getting to drive. Eventually I got to drive to school, and, being a teenager, I drove like an idiot. There was a circle in the school between the band department and the gym, designed to give parents more parking places for picking up kids after activities.

And being an idiot teenager, I was showing off and went around the circle at a fairly high speed in my grandfather's '55 Chevy. The tires were squealing, and everyone was looking, as I wanted them to do, when I slid across the slippery vinyl seat until I hit the right door. It is very difficult to control a left-hand-drive car from the right-hand seat.

Fortunately, the stick-shift car, in second gear, had enough engine braking to slow it down when my foot left the throttle, and I was able to scamper over to the driver's seat and regain control before I did anything any more embarrassing than I already had, avoiding the quickly looming curb.

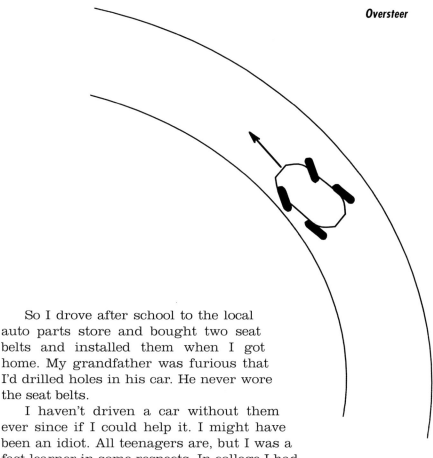

So I drove after school to the local auto parts store and bought two seat belts and installed them when I got home. My grandfather was furious that I'd drilled holes in his car. He never wore the seat belts.

I haven't driven a car without them ever since if I could help it. I might have been an idiot. All teenagers are, but I was a fast learner in some respects. In college I had a '65 Mustang, and I put in a racing harness, a three-inch-wide belt with a two-inch shoulder harness, and when autocrossing I noticed how much better I could control the car because I didn't move around. This didn't surprise me. Roger Ward, the great Indianapolis 500 driver had come to our school on a pro-seat belt campaign and mentioned that when he went to Monza for the 1955 Race of Two Worlds the Americans had seat belts in their cars. The Europeans didn't. He had gotten the pole and mentioned to some of the Europeans the advantage of seat belts holding him in place and enabling him to control the car better. One of them put seat belts in his car and outqualified him.

Until good, retractable three-point belts (meaning one shoulder belt, one lap belt, and three-point mounting) became standard equipment on every car, I put in various competition belts on my street machines over the years despite the funny looks from superiors and cops at traffic stops. The three-point belt was invented by Volvo engineer Nils Bolin in the fifties and is now equipped with perfected inertia reel retractors and, in some cars, pyrotechnic emergency tensioning retractors. It is an added bonus to have pyrotechnic, not mechanical, emergency tensioning retractors. In a crash exceeding 3 Gs deceleration, equivalent to hitting an immovable wall at 13 mph, the ETR will tighten the seat belt six to seven inches. Since in a more severe crash your body weight will stretch the belts several inches, this is a real plus in keeping you in place.

Adjust the seat height accordingly, too. You should give yourself as much survival room as possible. That means as low a seating position as you can still see over the hood. In a rollover even the best of cars will show some roof damage. If it only depresses four or five inches, you don't need it to depress into your head. On the other hand, shorter people need a height-adjustable seat so they can raise it up high enough to see effectively.

Understeer, Oversteer, Front and Rear Wheel Skids

Eventually if you push a car, you will determine that it doesn't, at the limit, go where it is pointed. This came as a shock to me.

Understeer occurs when a car does not turn at as sharp an angle as the steering wheel movement should generate. In severe understeer the front end of the vehicle loses traction and tends to "plow" ahead into the curve. Both for liability reasons and good sense, most cars are designed to exhibit moderate understeer in normal driving. However, on slippery surfaces, and with the right provocation, most cars can be made to oversteer under certain circumstances.

Oversteer occurs when a car turns with a sharper angle than the input to the steering wheel should generate. This condition can result in the rear end of the car losing traction and sliding outward. This isn't usually considered desirable on the street. In fact, when it occurs it's usually a high pucker factor condition. Oversteer, it has been said, is what your car did just before the spin.

Oversteer

If your car enters a corner too fast and it understeers, you will hit the tree with the front bumper. If it oversteers, or if you've provoked oversteer through poor weight transfer, you will hit the tree with the rear bumper.

Race cars need oversteer. An oversteering car is called loose. An understeering car is said to push. It is said loose is fast. Having said that, if you're driving a car that oversteers in normal driving, either (a) get it fixed, or (b) trade it in. (And if you are going racing, start with a setup of mild understeer until you've gotten as fast as you can with that setup. If you can handle that, perhaps more looseness is called for, but beginning racers too often go for the fastest setup and then can't control it.)

Weight transfer can turn a normally understeering car into an oversteering car. If you're saying to yourself, Weight transfer? Come on, the weight isn't going to move on the car. This doesn't make sense. Actually, it does. When I talk about weight, it's the weight on the four little-bitty patches of rubber that connect you to the road. When you brake, the weight on the tires is shifted forward, and when you accelerate, it's shifted rearward. If you lurch right, the weight will shift to the left wheels, and if you lurch left, it'll shift to the right wheels.

Notice the next time you drive, when you accelerate away from a stoplight the weight transfers to the rear. The nose comes up. The rear of the car squats. You're pushed back in your seat. Then, when you approach a traffic light that turns yellow, then red, causing you to brake hard, the nose goes down, the tail comes up, and you are thrown forward in your seat. Loose objects in the car slide forward. This is weight transferring forward.

If you need to make a violent evasive maneuver, say, to turn left to avoid the truck that just fell out of the sky right in front of you, if you brake and turn, the additional weight on the front wheels will make them very effective, and the front of the car will turn very smartly. The rear tires, unloaded, meaning relieved of weight by the weight transfer, won't have enough contact pressure to maintain traction, and they will slide. The result will be a rear-wheel skid—possibly, if uncorrected, a spin.

If, on the other hand, you plant your right foot down hard, the weight will be transferred to the rear wheels, and they will get a good bite. The fronts won't be as effective in turning the car, so it won't respond as quickly. Then you'll be able to steer around the object, and, if another car is now heading at you head on, steer back into your lane.

If you jam on the brakes and lock them up, a locked wheel does not steer, and you hit the truck. But as the twenty-first century is approaching, you aren't buying any cars without anti-lock brakes, are you?

Sometimes you want to transfer weight. Sometimes you don't. Usually as little weight transfer as possible is desirable. The smoother you are with your controls, the less you will transfer weight.

If the car is in a front-wheel skid, meaning the front wheels aren't grabbing, and the car is understeering off the road, the cure is to take your foot off the throttle. Ultimately, if you've entered a corner too fast and the car is understeering, there's little you can do to cure it. But most people's reaction is to slow down when the car starts to plow, and that cures it. Another reason a racing car should have some oversteer is because oversteering, or a rear wheel skid, can be controlled by an expert.

Normally, when the rear wheels skid the proper response is to add a little steering input, turning the wheel in the direction to straighten the car out. Sometimes backing off on the throttle will make the skid worse. Remember, when you back off the throttle the weight transfers forward, unloading the rear tires. Unloaded tires have less grip, and the skid worsens. If the skid is caused by excessive application of power to the rear wheels of a rear-wheel-drive car, then backing off the throttle just a tad is good. If it's an old Porsche 911, a rear-engined car with a serious tendency toward oversteer, and you've induced oversteer, you'd better steer out of it quickly. Driving an older 911 Porsche takes a lot of sensitivity and feel.

On a track, powering a car around a corner until the tail hangs out a bit, meaning the rear wheels have just begun to lose adhesion, meaning you're at the limit, makes sense. Doing this on the street, unless you're being chased by the hounds of hell, doesn't. Even then, as we'll see, it isn't a great idea.

If all four wheels are right at the limit of adhesion and sliding a bit, this is a four-wheel drift. Four-wheel drifts are definitely for racing cars. If you're drifting on the street a lot, please burn this book. When you kill three nuns and are being sued by the entire world, I don't want to be dragged in because they found my book in the wreckage.

Spin Control

A spin normally occurs when a rear-wheel skid is uncorrected, so the best way to avoid spins is to avoid rear-wheel skids. When the tail slides out, correcting by turning the wheel to straighten the car out—if you do it quickly enough and accurately enough—should correct it. If you're a fraction late, it won't. I remember sitting in a car driven by a young woman. She hit a patch of slippery stuff on a curve. The tail came out. She corrected a quarter-second late and started a counter skid. She corrected that a quarter-second late, and another opposing skid resulted. She corrected that one a half-second late, but it had gone past 90 degrees, and the car spun off the road into a barbed-wire fence.

When a rear-wheel skid goes beyond 90 degrees, it turns into a spin. If the car is pointed backward, straighten the steering wheel, and, if spinning has used up enough momentum, the car will continue down the road backward. At this point, if you have a manual transmission, the clutch should be depressed. With an automatic, you should get into neutral. Otherwise, with the car going backwards, the rear wheels will start turning backwards, which will make the engine turn backwards, and valves will hit pistons, and it can get expensive.

At the racing schools, the instructors will teach you, "When you spin, both feet in," meaning left foot depresses the clutch, right foot depresses the brakes. You want to declutch to keep the engine from blowing, and you want the brakes on to slow the car as much as possible.

Besides, driving down the road backwards is frowned upon by most law enforcement agencies and racing organizations. And it's really hard to steer. If the car is going backward, spin the wheel to full lock, and the car should spin on around until it is facing forward again. At this point, straighten the steering wheel. You can actually let it slide between your hands as it will try to straighten out naturally. If it's going forward then, you can drop it into the appropriate gear and continue down the road. Watch films of either Jimmy Clark, or later Danny Sullivan, at Indianapolis. Both spun at Indy, caught it, continued, and won the race.

A friend of mine spun one night on a rainy road, caught it, and continued, thinking pretty highly of his car control skills until he came to the town he had just left. It's best to catch it and continue in the direction you were going, not the opposite direction.

Smoothness

The secret of going fast is smoothness and precise control. Smoothness is the most important high-performance driving technique. I'll repeat: The most important high-performance driving technique is smoothness. Every racing driver knows this. Virtually every nonperformance driver doesn't. You want to go fast? Drive smoother.

This is where the uninformed driver says, "Yeah, right! Now tell me the real secret."

I just did. Believe it. You might think riding with a racing driver driving your car would be a wild ride. The wild part would be the cornering speeds and the late braking. But if it isn't a smooth ride, it's slow.

Why? Cornering, accelerating, and braking are all functions of those four little patches of rubber separating you from the road, your tire patches. The tires can do only so much. They might be capable of cornering at 1.05 Gs or braking at 1.05 Gs or accelerating at 1.05 Gs (assuming you had enough power, which you probably don't).

So if you go from accelerating to braking to cornering smoothly, you can go from 1.05 Gs braking and 0 Gs cornering to 1.05 Gs cornering, 0 Gs braking, 0 Gs accelerating. But if you are rough on the brakes and in your transition to cornering you jerk something, then the G force will spike in a direction you don't want it to, overloading the tire, and you'll either scrub off speed or lose adhesion and fall off the course, do a lurid slide, embarrass yourself, etc.

Teaching smoothness is difficult. I've switched seats with students and demonstrated. If they could tear their minds away from the fact that I was cornering their vehicle faster than they ever did, which was scaring the hell out of them, they might get the message. If they didn't, at Texas World Speedway they usually spun at a particular point. There's a right-hand turn on the road course followed by a left-hand turn that is slower. So in the transition between right and left, you need to brake briefly, downshift, and then corner. The braking and downshifting have to be done while the car is going straight during the transition period, or the car will spin. The downshift must be smooth, or the

Late apex turn

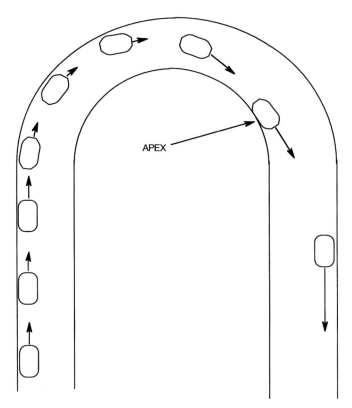

APEX

car will spin. The transition from braking to cornering must be done smoothly or the car will spin. If the student got it sideways there but not enough to spin, and I thought he hadn't gotten the message, I'd take him into the pit lane, change seats with him, and demonstrate. Then I would let him try again. Some took all weekend to get acceptable smoothness. Others never did. One or two spun there, usually putting the car outside of turn four, which was embarrassing at best. We would then black flag the poor devil when he got back on the road and let him explain his error to a steward in the pits. If he did it more than twice, anywhere on the course, he would have to explain to the chief instructor why he shouldn't be grounded for the weekend. One time, I never could get the message across to a student in a Pantera, not an ideal car to learn on, and he spun three times. I suggested perhaps I wasn't teaching correctly, and gave him to another instructor in lieu of grounding him. He had one more lurid spin to end his weekend. Both instructors breathed a sigh of relief.

Part of the reason that teaching smoothness is difficult is the student's natural desire to go fast. If you give the average enthusiast the exercise to go through a course at 35 mph and develop smoothness, the tendency is to cheat and push the car faster and faster until the in-

54

structor notices, calls him aside, and slows him down. Frequently, this doesn't apply to women. Not being cursed with an overabundance of testosterone, most of them will complete the exercise at the stated speed, and they will thus learn faster than the men who have to unlearn before they can learn. Unlearning is much more difficult than learning.

There are exercises to improve smoothness. Some you can do all of the time. When you are driving, practice smoothness. Practice upshifts and downshifts that are smooth and practice braking with even deceleration. Approach a stop sign and try to stop precisely on the spot intended with one smooth, constant braking motion ending in the car stopping without that little dip in the nose at the end.

Jackie Stewart teaches smoothness by taping a fairly flat salad bowl to the hood and putting a tennis ball in it and having the student go as fast as he can through a slalom (autocross) course. Of course the goal is to go through quickly without losing the tennis ball. This would make a good Sunday event for a car club. You may not learn smoothness this way, but you'll certainly learn that you *aren't* smooth.

When you're driving on the street a passenger shouldn't be able to feel your shifts, if you're shifting manually. And they really shouldn't be able to tell whether you're accelerating slightly, coasting, or braking slightly. Obviously, if you have to accelerate or brake hard, they'll notice. Smoothness has to come first, then speed.

Remember that: smoothness first, then speed.

The next two exercises come from Denise McCluggage.

Drive as if you have no brakes. Now don't get cute and run into a stopped Peterbilt. But if you accelerate gently and let the car coast as much as possible, it'll get smoother. You won't pull up behind the car in front of you in traffic, because when he slows down you'll have to use your brakes. Done right you can do this in your normal, everyday driving, and no one will notice.

Another exercise is to make sure you do nothing you'll have to undo soon. If you're accelerating, and cars ahead are stopping, you'll just have to brake soon, so accelerate more gently and coast down as much as possible. This way you're keeping the transitions smooth.

Remember the little toy dogs you used to see in the rear parcel shelf of some cars, the ones whose heads bobbed as you drove? ("Not my car," you say; "I never did that!") I didn't either. Imagine that you have one in the passenger seat with you, and if the head bobs, the car will explode. See how long you can drive without having the car blow up on you.

Today when you drive to or from work, try to simply drive as smoothly as possible all the way. If your normal route is sitting in the freeway at 0.001 mph, try taking the longer surface street route with all of the stop signs and traffic lights and turns. Since you have accepted the fact that you will take longer to get home, speed is no longer important, so changing lanes 30 times per mile isn't required (as if it ever was), and you can concentrate on operating the controls smoothly.

If you're not interested in motorsports, force yourself to watch a Formula 1 race. You might enjoy it. Note the in-car shots. The steering wheel will be moving from kickback. Ignore that. Notice how smooth the driver is. In the early days of in-car shots I watched Ayrton Senna qualify for the pole at Monte Carlo with a complete lap from inside the cockpit. It was phenomenal. The smoothness was visible. Jimmy Clark, an era earlier, was so smooth you couldn't tell whether he was accelerating or braking from another car. Michael Schumacher is like that today.

Basic Cornering

As you approach a corner, do your braking in a straight line. Remember the bit about the tire patches. If you're braking at 1.05 Gs, and that's the limit of the tires, if you start to turn, something's going to happen you don't want to happen.

Braking should be done as late as possible, of course. The end of the straight is where speed is made. If you brake 50 feet later than your opponent, you have gone those 50 feet at a high rate of speed. At 120 mph, you're moving at 176 feet per second. You've gained .28 second. Do that for 10 laps, and you've gained 2.8 seconds, 100 laps, 28 seconds. Do that on every corner, and pretty soon you'll be lapping your opponent. If it's someone chasing you, he'll be farther behind.

As you release pressure on the brake pedal, you can begin to turn in toward the apex. If you're still braking as you feed in steering, back off the brakes in the same amount you feed in steering. This is called trailing brake. The trick is to use trailing brakes to help the car corner.

What's An Apex?

The apex of the corner is the point at which your car is closest to the inside edge of the usable road available to you. I say "usable road available to you" because on the street you might only have the right side of the road. It's usually poor form to use the entire road with traffic oncoming.

You'll begin a corner using all of the available road. If you're turning left, move to the right verge before your turn-in point. Turn in smoothly. With most cars you'll want a late apex so you can get on the power sooner.

Early Apex

The cause of early apexing is turning in too soon.

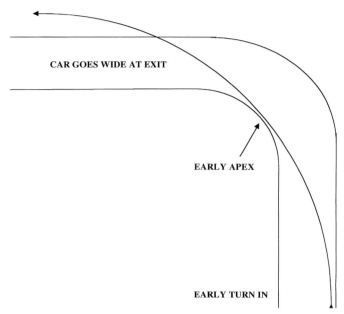

Late Apex

You'll see guys at races wearing T-shirts saying, "Friends don't let friends early apex." This is because an early apex results in your falling off the road at the exit of the turn or having to slow drastically to prevent it.

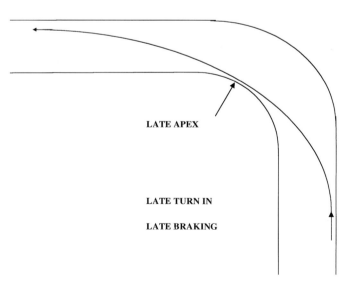

The Exit

Exiting the corner is where you make time. Ideally you want to get the power down (*smoothly*) as soon as possible. Get the power down 0.10 second sooner, and it'll translate to a car length at the end of a straight. Accelerate sooner, brake later, corner smoothly. Sounds simple. It is, but it isn't easy. As you put down power, gently unwind the steering, and the car will go toward the outside edge of the road. When it has straightened out and is against the outside edge of the road under full throttle, you've exited the corner. You should, by now, be set up for the next corner if you're on a race track. If you're on the street being pursued by the hounds of hell, the same thing applies, if you know where the next corner is, and you should.

If you're going from one corner to another, compromises have to be made to get the maximum speed out of all of the corners combined. It might, for example, be good to take the first corner a little slower in order to exit the second corner faster. Remember, speed is gained on the entrance and the exit.

Slow In, Fast Out

If you enter a corner too fast and make it around, you will have to scrub off speed in the corner, and you will exit going slow. If you enter a bit too slow, you will be able to accelerate early and will be able to salvage the corner, and at the next corner, you will be going quickly. Obviously it is better to be too slow coming in than too fast. Stirling Moss said, "I'd rather be slow in and fast out than fast in and dead out."

Tenths

Let's divide cornering potential into tenths. If the fastest the car can possibly be driven around a corner by an expert is, for the car, 10/10, and the fastest you can drive that car around a corner is, for you, 10/10, then 10/10 should be reserved for a track where going 10.1 /10 and thus falling off the road won't hurt you or the car. Going 10/10 on Red Mountain Pass near Ouray, Colorado, with 7,000-foot drops is probably a poor idea. In fact, on the street, 8/10 is probably dangerous. If you're being chased, you probably want to be at 8/ to 9/10 as we'll discover, no more.

The Impossibility of Cornering to Limits on the Street

Except for using the "line," you can't practice cornering on the street. (And the line has to be practiced within your lane!) The car is capable of tremendous cornering. There are street cars with street tires capable of doing 1 G corners. Do that on the street and the best thing that'll happen to you is you'll get arrested. This cornering should be done on a racetrack or an autocross track. For one thing, especially at an autocross track, there will be a safe runoff area. If you overcook and spin spectacularly, the only damage will be to your pride, a few cones, and possibly your tires.

Autocrossing for Practice and Skill Development

I would start on an autocross track, which is probably a parking lot. The Sports Car Club of America's regions do local autocrosses as often as once a month. The first thing to do is find out when and where the next autocross is. If, at the beginning of the season, they have an autocross school, sign up for it.

Most clubs have loaner helmets, and those that don't usually have someone who will loan his. So all you have to do is show up with your car. Clean the trunk out before you go and pump up the tires at least to the high speed pressures. If you keep a lot of stuff in the car, leave it at home. When I autocrossed I put all of the "stuff" I kept in the glovebox into a plastic bag so that I could take it out and put it back easily. I carried a large tarp and unloaded my spare tire, tools, and the contents of the car there. If it rained I folded the tarp over the stuff to keep it dry. I carried a lunch and a cooler of cold drinks.

Beyond Autocrossing, Driving Schools

After you have enough autocrosses and autocross schools under your belt to want any more, you should attend one or more driving schools. Schools range from inexpensive ones in which you bring your own car and helmet to schools like the Bob Bondurant School of High Performance Driving, where you bring yourself, your clothes, and tennis shoes. Of course, these schools cost more and take up more time.

The Porsche Club of America has schools and lapping sessions at racetracks all over the country. Some require Porsches. Some don't. It depends on their insurance and the number of Porsche drivers who sign up. The cost is not excessive, a couple hundred dollars in entry fees plus your expenses, and you're in. Beginners will be students. Experienced drivers will be allowed to lap by themselves. Students will be divided into two groups, beginners and former students. Normally four days (two weekend sessions) will be required as a minimum before a student will "graduate" and be allowed to lap by himself.

Your car must pass a technical inspection, and you must have a good quality Snell-approved helmet. Expect to pay $300 or more for a good helmet. Long sleeves are required, but Nomex driving suits are not. Before you go through technical inspection, it's probably a good idea to replace your brake pads and put in new brake fluid. Brake fluid degrades over the course of time, and you won't notice how soft your brakes have become until you replace your fluid. Brake fluid is hygroscopic, meaning it picks up water, which, of course, boils when hot, causing severe brake fade.

Preregistration and pretechnical inspection are required. Show up at the track early and expect to spend the morning of the first day in a ground school. Then, when you go on the track, the instructor will first drive your car, showing you the line and braking and shifting points. Then he will let you drive. When he tells you to keep the speed down and concentrate on the line and smoothness, keep the speed down and concentrate on the line and smoothness. You can't learn it all at once. Learn as much as you can each lap. Listen to what he is saying. Failure to listen was the worst problem I encountered.

Other Driving Schools

After some driving experience, autocrossing, PCA schools, and SCCA autocross schools, you might want more training. Or you might want professional training right now, skipping all that stuff. I recommend formal school training. In fact, I'm one of those oddballs who thinks every young person, at the appropriate age, should take the Bob Bondurant 2 Day Teen Defensive Driving Course in order to get an unrestricted license. (I'm sure Mr. Bondurant thinks so, too. He could buy a bigger, faster helicopter.) The Teen Driving Course was started because parents would ask about sending Junior, and Bondurant would recommend the 2 Day High Performance Driving Course, but some parents balked at sending their kids to anything with the words High and Performance used together (or even separately). So Bob redid the course for teenagers. Were I king, kids would need to take this course (after the required six months of street driving) before upgrading their learner's permits to full-fledged licenses.

The Sports Car Club of America has driving schools, but they're for racing only and are required for a racing license. (Some professional schools can now qualify one for an SCCA license.) But SCCA schools are interested in the technical minutiae of racing, how to go through tech, how to grid up, what the flags mean, etc. Each instructor will be assigned several students who drive the same sort of car he does. But he can't watch them all, and his sessions with each student will be brief and perfunctory. You will need a full-fledged SCCA race car, which can be rented, but the expense is not justified unless you want an SCCA racing license. For the purpose of this book, which is enlightened street driving, SCCA racing schools are not the way to go.

The country has a lot of good driving schools. I recommend, for non-racers, ones that use streetable automobiles. Learning in an open-wheeled Formula Ford (or Formula Dodge at Skip Barber) is great for racetrack skills, but road skills are more important and, more to the point, the object of this exercise. If you're hell-bent on racing, you'll take the schooling you need and go racing. It's the person who isn't hell-bent on racing, who doesn't particularly care about high-performance driving, who needs the kind of training in the Bondurant 2 or 3 Day High Performance Driving Course.

Another reason I recommend the Bondurant school is that all of his basic schools include skid control and the accident avoidance simulator. They have schools from a half-day to the 4 day Road Racing Course. Whatever you do, don't take the four-day course. It's so much fun you'll want to go racing.

I recommend the three-day course because it's all done in more-or-less streetable cars—Rousch-prepared Mustangs, which might be faster and rougher than the family Taurus, but they have fenders and behave like street machines. Also, the instructor can sit with you and tell you what you're doing wrong. Courses that use only single seat racing cars are fun, but it's harder to correct mistakes, and the training is usually most applicable to racetrack situations.

The 4 day Road Racing Course spends the last day and a half in Formula Fords, and this, I'll admit, is a lot of fun.

Schools That Teach High-Performance Road-Oriented Driving

The Skip Barber Racing School and Dodge/Skip Barber Driving School

29 Brook Street

Lakeville, CT 06039

(860) 435-1300

(800) 221-1131

www.skipbarber. com

The Skip Barber Racing School operates at 20+ tracks around the country. Skip Barber had been a successful Formula 5000 and Formula 1 driver who set out to teach enthusiasts the art and science of racing and driving technique. He created a step-by-step curriculum of driving skill development and provided his students with professional coaching and expert feedback, enabling them to advance much more rapidly than they could on their own. The school was started in 1975. The emphasis is on racing courses, using Formula Dodge open wheel single-seaters similar to the Formula Fords used by other schools. The Dodge/Skip Barber Driving School has courses using Viper GTS Coupes, Dakota V8 Sport trucks, ACR Neons, and Viper Roadsters in One or Two Day Dodge/Skip Barber Driving Schools, and they've just added a half-day course. Of the 20+ racetracks around the country at which the school's courses are offered, Lime Rock Park in Connecticut, Laguna Seca Raceway in California, and Road America in Wisconsin offer them only at the infield facilities.

The Half-Day Driving School covers threshold braking and skid control. Key classroom subjects include weight transfer and other essential vehicle-dynamics theory.

The One-Day Driving School teaches vehicle dynamics, slides and recoveries on the skid pad, threshold braking, and accident-avoidance maneuvers. The skills and knowledge learned here are combined in an autocross exercise using the Dodge Viper.

The Two-Day Driving School adds heel-and-toe downshifting, emergency lane changes, and accident-evasion techniques to the one-day curriculum as well as a classroom session on road manners. Two-Day graduates are eligible to enroll in the Car Control Clinic.

The Car Control Clinic is a one-day program conducted on a skidpad and short autocross course where you are encouraged to take the car beyond the limit. The Car Control Clinic acclimates you to the feeling of sliding, drifting, and rotating the car. Car Control Clinics are open to graduates of accredited racing schools and Dodge Skip Barber Two-Day Driving school graduates.

Bob Bondurant School of High Performance Driving
P. O. Box 51980
Phoenix, AZ 85076-2980
(520) 796-1111
fax: (520) 796-0660
http://www.bondurant.com
(800)-842-RACE (7223)

This is one of the oldest schools in the country. Bob Bondurant was first a motorcycle racer, then switched to cars in 1956, driving a Morgan. In 1959 he won the Corvette driver of the year award. In 1963 he joined Carroll Shelby's Ford Cobra team and won races, moving to Europe for the 1964 GT Championship. Paired with Dan Gurney, Bondurant won the GT category and fourth overall in the 24 Hours of Le Mans in a Ford Cobra Daytona Coupe.

In 1965 Bondurant won 7 out of 10 races and won the World Manufacturers' Championship in a Cobra. He also drove a Ferrari Formula 1 car for the factory Ferrari Team in the 1965 U.S. Grand Prix at Watkins Glen. In 1966 he continued in Formula 1 and drove for Ferrari in World Manufacturers' Championship events.

Additionally, he served as a technical consultant for John Frankenheimer's movie, *Grand Prix*. He was responsible for training the actors James Garner, Yves Montand, and Brian Bedford.

In 1967 the steering arm broke on his McLaren Mk II Can-Am car at over 150 mph, causing a crash, which injured him severely. At the time he thought he might never walk again and decided if he were able, he would like to start a school and teach others to drive.

In 1968 he started the Bob Bondurant School of High Performance Driving at Orange County International Raceway near Los Angeles. The first week he had three students. The second week, he had two, Paul Newman and Robert Wagner, training for the movie *Winning*. Bondurant was technical adviser for the film, taught the actors, and drove the camera car. Newman went on to be quite a successful racing driver, as did James Garner. As did a considerable number of his students who weren't celebrities.

The school moved first to Ontario Motor Speedway, then to Sears Point International Raceway. An agreement with Ford provided vehicles and technical support. In 1990 Bondurant moved to Phoenix, to a 60-acre facility with a 1.6 mile racetrack, 3.5-acre asphalt pad, handling oval, classroom and garage facilities with special skid cars, and more than 150 specially prepared Fords.

The school offers the Grand Prix Road Racing course, Advanced Road Racing, High Performance driving (2 and 3 days), Teenage Defensive Driving, Highway Survival Training, Executive Protection/Anti-Kidnap Driving, Corporate/Team Building Programs, and SCCA Regional Licensing.

The Highway Survival Training, one day, will teach you accident avoidance, panic-stopping, and skid control. This really should be required for a license instead of the way they're given out in Wheaties boxes.

Advanced Teenage Defensive Driving, one or two days, teaches accident avoidance, skid control, advanced braking and ABS techniques—active driving techniques that could someday save their lives.

Derek Daly Racing School

7000 N. Las Vegas Blvd.
Las Vegas, NV 89115
(702) 643-2126, 1 (888) Go-Derek
http://www.speedcentre.com

This school, located in Las Vegas, has a one-day car control clinic in addition to its pure race-oriented courses, which are done in formula cars.

Driving Dynamics

25 Bridge Avenue
Red Bank, NJ 07701
(908) 219-0404

Driving Dynamics has one- and two-day Advanced Driving Schools in New Jersey, SCCA Accredited two-day Performance Schools at Pocono Raceway, corporate driver development programs around the world, team-building and awards programs, and anti-terrorist and anti-carjacking programs. Programs include skid control training on the Driving Dynamics controlled slide car. Mobile classrooms are available for corporate and group training anywhere in the United States. Two-day programs at Pocono include a performance driving school followed by a day in your car on one of Pocono's road courses. One-on-one instruction is also available.

Car Guys, Inc.

P. O. Box 21275
Roanoke, VA 24018
(800) 800-4897

Car Guys has schools all over the country: Sebring, Charlotte, Atlanta Motor Speedway, Watkins Glen, Summit Point, Roebling Road, etc. But the student brings his own car. Thus the cost is low, if you don't count tire wear and the cost of stuffing the family sedan into the wall. Prices range from $295 to $395 for a two-day school.

Car Guys also offers for corporate or governmental safety training their Decisive Driving Car Control program, featuring the Michelin Mobile Skid Control Lab and Accident Avoidance System. Classes are offered regularly in Manassas, Virginia. In addition, the program is fully mobile and can be administered at clients' sites.

Obviously, cost and location factors will determine what training you can acquire. Students traditionally save their pennies for some time and choose one school. Having had training from several schools, I can recommend getting as much as you can. Possibly a basic course followed by one of the anti-kidnap, anti-carjacking schools is a good idea if the risk is great enough.

CHAPTER FIVE

AVOIDING THE CRAZIES

Most of the people out there are just like you. Isn't that a scary thought? "You mean I'm just like them? That's an insult!" No, not really. Most of the people out there are just trying to get where they're going. They're frustrated at the traffic. They wish they were driving a nicer car, or they wish other people would respect their nice car more. They're not dangerous. They might be driving over their heads and be only semi-competent to handle emergencies (and the rest are totally incompetent to handle emergencies). But they're generally just folks trying to get along on the road enough to get home, to work, to the lake, etc. But as stress increases, the stress of traffic congestion, too many rats in a box, they do things they wouldn't do without the anonymity of the automobile around them, the same as people in New York City and Chicago, overcrowded to the point of insanity, behave more rudely than people in small towns where everyone knows them.

Then there's that three percent. In the military we used to say, "There's always that three percent that didn't get the word." These are the guys whipping through 50 mph traffic at 80, changing lanes like they were in a video game. They're the ones who exit the freeway from the left lane or turn left from the right lane. They're the ones who snap one day and start bumping the guy who cut them off, or follow him till he stops and start pummeling him.

Incident 3

A delivery truck and a pickup truck had a minor fender bender. The pickup truck driver tried to exchange information with the delivery truck driver without success, so he went back to his car and began to call the police. The delivery truck driver, who, unknown to the pickup truck driver, was on probation for accidents and would lose his job if another were reported, told the pickup truck driver not to make the call. The pickup truck driver continued to make the call. The delivery truck driver went to the other's truck and began to beat him, breaking his jaw, and endangering the much smaller man's life. With his consciousness ebbing, the pickup truck driver retrieved a pistol and fired one shot at his attacker, killing him and saving his own life. A grand jury no-billed him.

Incident 4

Early Road Rage: In the ill-fated Donner party one afternoon one wagon passed another wagon while climbing a hill. This so enraged the driver of the wagon passed that he stabbed the driver of the other wagon to death.

Incident 5

The woman was upset with the car in front of her. He was going 30 mph in a residential area, and she was in a hurry. So she passed him on the right at a stop sign. She was surprised when he began to tailgate her and followed her for several miles, cursing. She began to get scared and leaned out of the window to shout to him to leave her alone when he rammed her car. He continued ramming her car until he put her off the road. He sped away as she crawled out of the wreckage.

Incident 6

The cop was in an unmarked, plainclothes car when a pickup truck came up from behind, flashing his lights and honking for him to move over and let him pass. The cop was driving 80 in a 55 zone, so he refused to move over. The pickup truck driver honked his horn and shot him the finger. The cop slammed on his brakes, causing the pickup truck driver to swerve. Now the pickup truck driver was next to him. The cop looked over at the other driver and was surprised to see him pointing a gun at him. He drew his own gun, and both started shooting. The other driver was killed, the cop was badly wounded. When the investigators arrived, they discovered both men were undercover cops. They assumed that something concerning their jobs had triggered the tragedy, that perhaps one was dirty, but the investigation concluded they didn't know each other, that "road rage" had triggered the event.

Incident 7

A woman driver, angry at the way another woman had barged into her lane, passed the "offender" on the shoulder, pulled in front of her, then spiked the brakes, sending the other driver out of control and into a parked 18-wheeler. She lost an unborn child. The woman who had tried to punish her was convicted of aggravated vehicular manslaughter.

Road Rage

In 1997, *USA Today, US News and World Report*, and *Newsweek* all had major stories about road rage. Barbara Walters raved on about it on 20/20. If you believe the liberal media, it's more of a threat than nuclear proliferation.

Road rage is not the cause for all crazed drivers. There were crazed drivers long before the term was coined by the liberal media. Most of what the media calls road rage is simply aggressive driving. It has become a cause celebre on TV and among liberal lawmakers who want even more control over our lives. The cure, according to them, is stricter enforcement of all traffic laws, zero tolerance. Zero tolerance is loved by politicians because it will bring in more revenue. But will it stop road rage?

The trick is to not become involved in road rage incidents or with other crazies, whether it's just incompetent drivers or aggressive drivers or homicidal drivers. Usually, the homicidal drivers aren't homicidal when they leave the house. They just have incredibly short fuses. Don't light them.

Basic Courtesy, What a Concept

At one point in time, driving to and from work was extremely stressful to me. I would have some sort of incident with another driver almost every day. A driver would do something incredibly rude or thoughtless or stupid, and I would let him know I thought he was incredibly rude or thoughtless or stupid, and he would disagree with that, and we would have tense moments.

Then one day I decided to stop playing. If an idiot turned left from the right lane in front of me, scaring me half to death and causing me to slam on the brakes, I would ignore him. If someone with no signal cut in front of me, I just slowed down a little to have a proper following distance and ignored him. If another idiot went out of his way to keep me from entering the freeway in front of him I just pulled in behind him. Odds are he was exiting soon and wouldn't impede my travel. So I ignored him.

If someone was trying to merge into the freeway, I would slow to let him in front of me. If he signaled that he wanted into my lane in front of me, I would slow and let him in. If someone tailgated me, I would just move over. It's amazing how less stressful the drive to and from work became.

So first drive using the golden rule, do unto others as you would have them do unto you. If you're polite to them, you won't be the trigger that makes them start spraying bullets. Don't expect them to be polite back. Remember, there is no head of the line. You can try to pass every car you encounter on the road, but there will always be another one in front of you.

Stop for red lights. Stop for yellow lights if you can do so without locking up the brakes or getting rear-ended. Someone on the other side is going to floor it as soon as his light turns green even if you're coming through. Set yourself above the incompetence. Drive competently and ignore the incompetent, and you'll get home with much less stress.

Concentration, Concentration, Concentration

Excuse me, what did you just say?

If you're concentrating on driving well, you'll see the guy running the red light or approaching from the rear at flank or weaving through traffic, and you can get out of his way ahead of time. I'm a believer in not changing lanes any more than I have to. Each lane change has its own dangers, and it angers other drivers for you to weave through traffic. So I stay put. If someone is weaving through traffic from behind, I move over and let him go. He might be a good rabbit—someone to deflect the revenue collectors from your car. An idiot driving badly doing 85 is a perfect rabbit if you can keep him in sight without being an idiot, too.

Passing on the shoulder, cutting in line, tailgating, changing lanes without signaling and cutting off drivers, weaving through heavy traffic to make three spaces in five miles, etc., will make you the target of road rage a lot more often than driving in a friendly manner. It will also raise your stress levels so you'll go postal one day and be guilty of road rage yourself.

The Crazy Tailgater

I've had a lot of trouble with this. It isn't road rage; its stupidity. The crazy tailgater sticks on your tail. He might be trying to use your radar detector because he doesn't have one. He might be trying to get you to move over. The problem is the same. I drive pretty fast on rural interstates without much traffic, and I get the radar detector tailgater a lot. I don't mind being used as a rabbit, but the idiots haven't read this book. If you're going to use someone as a rabbit, give him at least 100 yards and preferably 500. I've tried all kinds of cures, and it hasn't been pleasant. Nothing works all of the time, but try this if you're being tailgated:

First, move over to the right lane. He may not pass you, but he might not follow you to the right lane. I've had them stay 20 feet behind me but still in the left lane. Then take your foot off the gas and let the car coast. If he's using your radar detector and you slam on the brakes, he'll think you've gotten a radar hit and will brake with you—if he doesn't hit you. But if you start coasting down, he will have a tendency to go around. If he doesn't, when you get 20 mph below the speed limit, put on your emergency flashers. If he's in hurry, he'll go around at this point.

Then you have the next problem. Does he go on at the speed you've been going, or does he go slower? Odds are out front by himself he won't go as fast as you were going. Now you have the choice of staying 100 yards behind him or trying to pass him again, only to have him tailgate you again.

Unless you've just gotten fuel, now might be a good time. If you were considering stopping for lunch, now might work. If you can do something to break up this unhealthy interstate relationship, do it.

Sometimes nothing works. I remember driving to a rally one time, and a car got on my tail. I tried all of the above tricks plus speeding to 130 mph to lose him, but when I coasted down he caught up and tailgated again. I finally coasted to a stop. He stopped behind me, flashers on. After some minutes I took off and exited and got gas. He followed me and got gas at the next pump. I explained that I would prefer if he didn't tailgate me, that he could follow if he wanted to if he'd give me 100 yards. He explained it was a free country and he liked my radar detector.

Finally, I took down the radar detector and put it in the trunk. Then I got on the freeway and set the cruise control to the speed limit, which, of course, virtually *no one* does. He sat behind me being passed by every car on the road for a good ten miles before he went on.

The problem with this cure is that I was the one slowed down. Unfortunately, dropping calthrops or an oil slick is frowned upon except in James Bond movies. Sometimes to get rid of tailgaters, though, you have to lose time. There is no good solution that the police will let us do.

In heavy traffic, drive at the speed limit. The road ragers and the crazies will go on. Don't block the left lane to do this. "Keep Right Except to Pass" is a law I respect. This will limit *your* road rage. Hurley Haywood, three-time winner of the 24-Hours of Le-Mans (and former One Lap of America contestant) made a pact with himself to drive to work at less than 50 mph because he was getting too mad. Now he doesn't get mad.

So You've Been Cut Off. What Do You Do?

Nothing. You're not the police, and if you are, you probably have bigger crooks to go after. Give him room. Get over it.

Consider Disconnecting Your Horn

People are getting killed for using their horns. I'm of the opinion that the horn button should be connected to a device that gives a painful electrical shock to the seat of the driver. Then if you *really* need to use your horn, you'll do so. But if you're using it to say, "Hey, idiot! I saw that!" you'll be better off not using it.

Incident 8

I was driving home one Friday afternoon down a two-lane street. As I approached a parking lot a Mustang with two teenagers pulled out in front of me. Reflexively, as I stood on the anti-lock brakes, I hit the horn. Both teenagers gave me a dirty look. I just missed hitting them. They didn't do anything to change their actions because of the horn—at least not to avoid the accident. Instead they made a U-turn on the heavily traveled road and ran several cars off the road chasing after me.

I was unaware of this due to the curves in the road until they appeared in my rearview mirror. They began tailgating me and making obscene gestures at me. Then, when the road became four lanes, they pulled even with me and displayed a cheap Tec-9 pistol, a big ungainly thing that looks like a submachine gun and holds a large magazine of 9 mm.

By then I was on the phone with the police. I turned right on a side street at a high rate of speed with no warning, losing them. Then I made three right turns to make sure they weren't following me and stopped and waited for a while before going home. As you would expect, the police were useless. The two teenagers were gang members, and they later used the Tec-9 in a murder of another gang member as he used a pay phone.

I had avoided the accident because of actions of my own. They had ignored the horn, but it caused them to behave in an insane manner. People have been murdered for using their horns. Use yours only if by using it you can prevent an accident, and be prepared to run like a rabbit when you use it.

Invisible Cars Don't Provoke Road Rage

I'm not saying that the victims of road rage deserve it. On the contrary, the crazies deserve more severe penalties than they get when they get caught, but to avoid crazies it's best to be as invisible as possible. Drive fast when there's no one around. When there's heavy traffic and the chance of more road rage, blend in.

The British Royal Automobile Club has a list of suggestions that might help:

The RAC Guide to Keeping Calm
1. Forget work or home worries while you are behind the wheel. Concentrate on your driving instead.
2. Plan your journey; it helps reduce anxiety and stress.
3. In-car entertainment can also help reduce stress, especially in traffic jams.
4. Don't try to change other people's attitudes to driving—you can't. But you can change your own.
5. Try to be courteous and stay calm if provoked by another motorist.
6. Drive with your doors locked and if you sense trouble, do not leave the safety of your car.

7. Count slowly from 1 to 10 if you are tempted to jump out of your car in a fit of rage.
8. Do not retaliate by flashing headlights, sounding your horn, or making rude gestures: It only makes a volatile situation worse.
9. If you are the victim of aggression, note the perpetrator's registration number and report the incident to the police immediately.

CHAPTER SIX

EVASIVE DRIVING TECHNIQUES

The First 10 Seconds

In Vietnam, we were taught the first 10 seconds of an ambush were the critical ones. This is even more critical in the peacetime civilian world. We were always in Condition Yellow, weapons at hand. In 10 seconds we could fire back 20 rounds per man plus a grenade, plus our automatic weapons and grenade launchers. You don't have that capability, but what you do when first attacked is the key to survival. If you're overcome by shock and surprise, as the attacker expects, he will win.

Panic Control

Panic kills more people than their attackers do. Panic can happen to anybody. I'd been in combat ten months and had been on an operation in Cambodia for three weeks when, after we had been resupplied and were walking to our night defensive position, firing started in front of me—close, but out of sight due to the deep forest vegetation. Not knowing what was going on but figuring we had been ambushed, I dived behind the biggest tree in close proximity, landing in a rank smelling mud puddle and covering myself with mud. To add to my panic, the safety of my rifle had rusted in place since the rifle had been cleaned the night before. My lieutenant was laughing at my panic. It was very embarrassing. But no one got hurt. It had been an ambush—a one-man ambush by an enemy soldier in khaki shorts with no weapon other than a grenade. He tossed it at one of my advisory team members and ran. My guy panicked and fired a magazine at him without hitting him. The grenade spoon had rusted in place, so he survived.

When I knew I was going into harm's way I was calm. It was the instant surprise that caused the one-time panic reaction. Other surprises didn't. The lieutenant? He had his own panic reaction when we were hit by friendly artillery, and I had to send him to the rear for a desk job. He had faced the tiger one time too many and that circuit in the brain that keeps men from curling into the fetal position and crying switched off.

When you're threatened or attacked, controlling panic is your first priority. The proper response is anger. If you're angry, you will survive—if you fight back intelligently.

Several predictable things will happen to you under adrenaline overload: You will lose control of the small muscles. Your fingers and hands will shake. The arm and leg muscles will work fine, but the fingers won't be as easy to control. Massad Ayoob researched this for his book *Stressfire*. He developed a shooting system designed to work while under extreme stress. Consider this to be Stress Driving.

Your vision will narrow, losing peripheral vision and becoming tunnel vision in extreme cases. You will be concentrating on the threat so heavily that a second assailant can sneak up behind you easily, and you might not see a friendly behind the threat. Remember that when shooting you hit what you are looking at, which explains the number of times people have shot their assailants at or around their guns. They're looking at them. When driving, you drive where you're looking. If you are trying to miss a car in an extreme driving maneuver, look where you want to go instead of at the car.

Your heart rate and respiration will go up. Your blood pressure will spike at levels that could kill a healthy person. This is why people have heart attacks under stress and were "scared to death." Your mouth will dry up, and you will have a desire to urinate, sometimes with difficulty controlling the impulse. People have lost bowel control as well. Breathing increases almost to a pant, sometimes causing hyperventilation with the symptoms of dizziness, numbness of extremities, and fainting.

Everything will s-l-o-w d-o-w-n. Suddenly everything will be in slow motion.

Auditory input might become limited. In gunfights people have reported not hearing the guns fire at all, or they seemed very quiet. Other people were surprised at how loud they were. I've experienced both phenomena at one time or another. Not hearing shouted warnings is common—and deadly if the warning is from a cop to put down the gun.

The body will dump massive amounts of adrenaline (epinephrine) into the bloodstream. Blood flow is diverted to the large muscle groups. The body is getting prepared to produce large amounts of energy. This will leave your hands and face pale, chalky white. Your hands will be cold and clammy.

With the loss of blood to the fine muscle groups, the body becomes clumsier. Trembling begins in the hands, weak hand first, next in the knees. "My knees were knocking" is usually a true statement, not just a figure of speech, after a period of extreme perceived danger.

Pain tolerance goes out of sight. Men in combat suffer terrible wounds and ignore them. They give medals for that, but sometimes they actually don't feel pain. A friend was shot in the leg in a firefight and said he noticed it after the firefight when his leg began to itch. When he noticed blood on his hand then he felt the pain.

You will fixate on small things. When Richard Davis, later the founder of Second Chance Body Armor Company, was shot by a robber, as he drove himself to the hospital he got considerable glee from the fact that he could drive as fast as he wanted to. He'd been shot, the perfect excuse for speeding.

Expect any or all of these things to happen—every time. If they don't, fine. Most of the time I was in combat these things didn't happen. The worst of them never happened to me, fortunately. (The loss of bowel control was just too embarrassing to contemplate. Perhaps the heavy rice diet of the Vietnamese troops protected me, and my bladder never failed me, either.)

But when I've been threatened in civilian life, out of practice and not expecting it, I've gotten the tachypsychia, the dry mouth, the sweaty palms, the shaky fine muscles. Using a cellular phone was difficult. Expect these symptoms, and you can deal with them. The unexpected is what terrifies us.

How to Know You're Being Followed

I've talked to several attack victims who never knew they were being followed, so they went home. Cornered there, they were robbed or raped or both. Assume someone is going to try to follow you every time you drive a car (or walk to your car in a parking lot). You're in Condition Yellow, right? You should notice a car following you. But he might be good, or you might be tired, and you might not notice it. Of course, when in doubt, make three right turns.

When you walk to your car in the parking lot always check the back of the car. If someone is planning on following you, he might make your car more identifiable by breaking a taillight or sticking on a piece of reflective tape. If I found either on my car I would assume I was being followed.

Don't park in the far edge of the parking lot in order to minimize door dings. Park as close in as you can and risk the door dings, but park between cars, not vans or big SUVs. Someone hiding in a van can open the door and grab you from behind when you start to get into your car. They can also hide under the van and grab your ankles as you stop to open your door. Worse, goblins have been known to slash the ankles of their victims, making it impossible for them to run away.

Most people are most vulnerable on their drives to and from work and their drives home. One of the things one does in high-threat environments is to vary one's schedule, to not leave for work or home at the same time. This isn't possible for most of us working stiffs. We have to be at work at 0730 every day. If you can't vary the schedule, you have to be extra vigilant. Before you go to the car, look out the window to see if anything sounds or looks strange. I mention sounds because if you live in a residential neighborhood with dogs in it, they will tell you if anything is amiss. It might just be a gardener next door, but the nearest dog will begin barking. Then the rest will. I pay attention to the dogs in my neighborhood. I figure out what they're barking at before dismissing it. Most of the times it's no threat. But if it is, they're trying to tell you.

If a thief notices your shiny gold Rolex watch at a bar and follows you for it, he's going to attack when you get out of the car at your home. If you've been at a bar, you're not likely to be in Condition Yellow. Here's one thing you can do on your drive home: There's a point in every drive home when you make a right turn. You make the same one every day. Force yourself *every* time to look and see if anyone makes the turn after you.

"So what? People go the same way I do all the time." Well, now you've noticed him. You're in Condition Orange. You're going to watch him. Is he still behind you after you make your next turn? Well, he could be going the same place legitimately. This is true. But when you get to your next-to-last turn before going down your street, decide if he's suspicious or not. If he is, *don't go home*. Make another turn in the same direction as the last one. Make one more if necessary to complete the three turns in the same direction in a row. If he follows you through three, he's following you. You have a problem, and you know it.

The Passenger Vanity Mirror

Most cars have vanity mirrors on the passenger's visor these days. If yours doesn't, buy a stick-on mirror and put it on the visor so your passenger can see it when the visor is folded down. Then your passenger can help watch for people and cars you've noticed and seem suspicious. The passenger can also manipulate the mirror to see things you can't without swiveling your head noticeably.

How to Lose a Tail

Call the police on your cellular phone as soon as you can. If he's just following and not chasing, drive to where the police tell you. If you can't reach the police by phone, head for the nearest police station. Lacking that, head for the nearest fire station. Pull up in front of the fire trucks and you're guaranteed to get the attention of several fit young men who are in the business of helping people. Try a hospital emergency room entrance. There are usually police there, and there will surely be someone to come out, even if it's just to tell you you're in a no-parking zone. Lacking one of those opportunities, head for the most public place you can find. Is there a full-service gas station around? If he's following you, he doesn't want witnesses, any witnesses. He will generally not follow you to any of those places.

One way to lose some tails is to slow for a yellow light then run just before the light turns red, making the tail have to run the red light. With most urban traffic, however, this is no sign he is tailing you, as usually three or four cars go through after the light turns red anyway, and this isn't suspicious.

Much more dangerous but almost guaranteed to lose the tail is to make an illegal left turn against oncoming traffic. You have to time it right, preferably when there's a string coming, just before the first of the string arrives, like so:

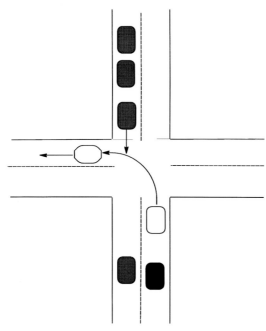

A good tail, a professional, will use a parallel street where possible. Real professionals will use two cars. This is more difficult to detect.

Parallel surveillance uses two or more vehicles. One vehicle tails the target at a respectable distance. His colleague follows on a parallel street ready to follow more closely should the target turn. This will not work in areas lacking parallel roads.

Leapfrog surveillance involves two vehicles, one closely following the target, the other well ahead of the target vehicle, the two tailing vehicles in radio contact with each other. The tailing vehicle can fall way behind while the lead vehicle slows and establishes visual contact with the target. The tailing and leading vehicles can change positions to avoid detection.

They also might put a bumper beeper on your car. A bumper beeper is an electronic tailing device. It attaches to the underside of the target car and sends a beeping signal to the receiving car. The most sophisticated have GPS locators on them. Less sophisticated models have a range of one to five miles. Some will beep differently if the target turns left than if it turns right. Usually they're battery-powered and attached with a magnet, though clamps and double-sided tape are also used. If you suspect such a tail, you should inspect the car every time you approach it. Feel and look under the bumpers for a small, magnetic device with one or two antennas. Sears sells a small rectangular mirror on an extendible handle, which is useful in checking under your car without getting stains on the knees of your clothes.

With a field strength meter (available at Radio Shack or the equivalent), with the ignition on, check around and under your car. The meter will help locate a transmitter. The average criminal following you home for your Rolex will not employ such a method. If you're the victim of such surveillance, you have a real problem. You are up against professionals. If you are a diamond broker, in the witness protection program, or have some other reason that would cause such surveillance, it's time to call in the cavalry, meaning professional help, whether it is the police or private security experts.

What If He's Chasing You:

If someone follows you through three turns of the same direction he's following you. Is he chasing you? Usually you won't know he's chasing you until he's made some attempt at running you off the road or produced a weapon or done something else that convinces you he's chasing you. If he's chasing you, really chasing you, not just angry with your driving but seriously threatening bodily harm, you have two priorities, in this order:

1. Don't crash

Keep it between the ditches. Most police chases end in crashes within five miles. Sometimes it's the chasee. Sometime it's the police car. Sometimes third parties are involved. Car chases are extremely dangerous. If a goblin is chasing you, it's even more dangerous. In a police chase at least one of the drivers might know what he's doing, and he can get more police to help him, helicopters, road blocks, etc. You probably don't have that luxury, plus it's much easier to chase than it is to be chased. If you're being chased, you have to decide when to turn, whether or not to run red lights, etc. He sees your brake lights, and your going through an intersection fast will alert other traffic that something's going on, and he might have an easier time getting through the intersection.

2. Don't let him catch you

It goes without saying that if the chaser isn't a danger to you, don't run. If you're carrying a princess and her lover, and the people chasing you are just photographers, let them follow you. A car chase is too dangerous to do unless it's a life-threatening situation. This chapter assumes the people chasing you are armed and dangerous with evil intent.

To accomplish both aims, drive fast and smooth. Smoothness combined with decisiveness are the keys. Remember, most chases end in crashes. If he's driving over his head and crashes, the chase is over. You've won. Calmly, as calmly as possible under the circumstances, drive the car as fast as conditions allow.

Brake late and decisively. Braking for a turn, then not taking the turn for one reason or another guarantees he'll close on you. As described in the chapter on basic high-performance driving, you want to brake late, using threshold braking and trail braking as necessary to get around the corner.

Your practice should include learning braking distances and cornering speeds for typical intersections at various speeds. For example, at the standard four-way intersection, how fast can you take the left-hand corner? The right-hand corner? Let's say it's 35 mph. How late can you brake from 50, 60, 70, 80 and make the corner? Can you do this well by sight-reading, or should you practice on deserted roads? If you practice, work up until you're cornering at 90 percent. Your target cornering speed shouldn't be higher than 90 percent, 9/10, as mentioned in the high-performance driving chapter. It's O.K. to go 10/10 on a racetrack, but not the street, even if you're being chased. The penalty for going 11/10 is too severe on the street.

Remember, the chaser didn't go to Bondurant. He may be aggressive, but it's unlikely he's well trained. Even if he's naturally skilled, an average driver with training can beat an untrained driver with above-average skills.

Use all of the available road. If the way is visible, this might mean using the whole road, but it probably means using just your side, but use two lanes of a four-lane road. Use the shoulder if it's smooth. If it's littered with debris you don't need to flatten a tire. Maybe he'll be tempted to use it and flatten his tires. Remember, don't crash. If he gets closer to you because he uses the left side of the road, endangering oncoming traffic, well perhaps you should keep making turns. He's in the most danger. As the movie character once said, "Risks are always risks." (*Grand Prix*, 1965) Your risks should be calculated. It's a calculated risk to drive within your limits and those of the road and traffic. It's more of a risk to exceed any of those.

Use the Strengths of Your Car Against the Weakness of His
Incident 9

Bill was driving through a rough neighborhood in Pasadena, Texas. He had been visiting relatives on Christmas Eve. A Chevrolet pickup driver, seeing his Mercedes, began to tailgate him and attempted to ram him twice. Bill knew if he stopped for a red light, the pickup would hit him. He ran a red light, emergency flashers on, and turned onto a freeway and accelerated. The pickup truck was accelerating for all it was worth. He knew he could outrun him, but soon he would hit traffic, and the pickup would catch up then. At 90 mph Bill could tell the pickup was beginning to shake. He stopped accelerating at 100 mph and let the pickup truck catch up, then accelerated a little more, then a little more until he was sure the pickup was doing its top speed. Chevrolet truck engines of that era would blow up if driven at top speed for any time. The oil return lines weren't big enough, and the oil would stay in the top end, starving the bearings. Bill let the pickup almost catch up. The driver began waving a pistol. Bill decided it was time to lose him and accelerated to 135 mph. He could see the pickup losing ground. Bill went over an overpass and watched for the pickup to appear. It didn't, and he slowed. Still no pickup. He assumed the pickup had blown its engine. He never knew why the pickup driver was chasing him.

If you're in a fast car, find a straight road and outrun him. If you're in a small, maneuverable car menaced by a pickup or SUV, look for a twisty road or a city street area so you can keep making turns till you lose him. If you're in the SUV menaced by a Corvette, go off road. Climb a curb and the fast sports car is lost. If you're in a Miata menaced by a Trans Am, look for the most turns you can accomplish. Your only chance is if he crashes or fades his brakes or blows his engine, all of which are more likely on a course with a lot of turns. Be creative.

Just don't drive like they do in TV chases. When I sold Chevrolets in the '70s, I saw several Camaros whose teenaged owners tried to mimic "The Rockford Files," and broke their cars in half at the firewall. Jumping cars doesn't work. Things break when they bottom. You can't go the wrong way down a crowded street, and when you run red lights, the other drivers aren't highly paid stunt drivers timing everything to the split second. You'll hit someone, or they'll hit you, and someone will die. Many police chases result in crashes involving innocent third parties.

When you crash, the person chasing you will either have you at his mercy or exit the scene. If he's trying to kill you, he will. If he's trying to rob you, he might, or he might exit the scene. If he exits the scene, you're now at fault in an accident. The police won't believe you were being chased. Do something really stupid, and you could be charged with vehicular manslaughter.

Trust me on the police-not-believing-you bit. Once a colleague was driving a

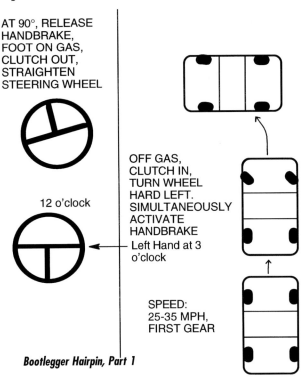

AT 90°, RELEASE HANDBRAKE, FOOT ON GAS, CLUTCH OUT, STRAIGHTEN STEERING WHEEL

12 o'clock

OFF GAS, CLUTCH IN, TURN WHEEL HARD LEFT. SIMULTANEOUSLY ACTIVATE HANDBRAKE
Left Hand at 3 o'clock

SPEED: 25-35 MPH, FIRST GEAR

Bootlegger Hairpin, Part 1

BMW trade-in. I don't know who owned it before, but he apparently had some enemies, and a van started tailing him. After making a few turns and not losing him, he called the police on the cellular phone and began to outrun him. He ran into a radar trap and stopped at the police car to report being chased. The van was right behind him going a high rate of speed. The policeman pulled him over, too.

The policeman ticketed the BMW driver for speeding. The driver explained the van was chasing him. It was pretty obvious, and he had just reported it to the 911 operator. The policeman asked the other driver if he was chasing the BMW. He said no. That ended that. He did give him a ticket, too, and he left the scene before the BMW did. The BMW driver asked for a jury trial, and the case was dismissed when the policeman failed to show up on trial date.

So unless the guy chasing you is also shooting at you, the risk of crashing exceeds the risk of his catching up, because if he catches up, there are still more options.

Evasive Maneuvers
The Bootlegger
Hairpin

This is the fun stuff, boys and girls (unless you have to do it for real and it's hairier than Don King with a Santa Claus beard).

Back in the '50s some of my relatives were said to be really good at this maneuver. They were running moonshine in Alabama and Tennessee. Then they started driving stock cars. The pay was better and the risk was less. The goal of the bootlegger's hairpin originally was to evade the ATF agents trying to catch them with moonshine. Before drugs, this was a problem for law enforcement in the

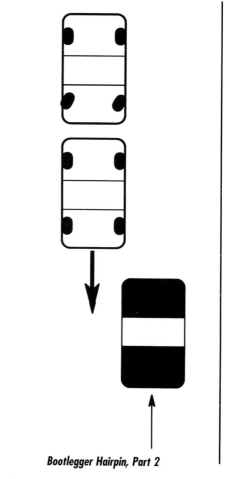

Bootlegger Hairpin, Part 2

Correct Skid with Counter Steering
Accelerate full throttle, headlights on bright, aim for left front of pursuer to try to run him off road.

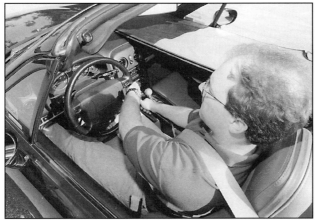

Steering-wheel hand position for the start of a bootlegger hairpin to the left. You've moved your left hand to the right as far as you can in preparation for spinning the wheel to the left. Car is in gear. When you start the maneuver automatics go to neutral, clutches go in on manual transmissions. Apply handbrake to maximum.

Steering-wheel hand position as you start the bootlegger hairpin. Left hand has spun the wheel to the left.

Steering-wheel hand position as you straighten the wheel. Release the handbrake. Let the steering self-straighten as you accelerate, first gear for manual, drive for an automatic. (Yes, you're doing a lot at once.) If you're really good, you won't have to shift an automatic into neutral, but if you're going backwards at this point, and you didn't, you'll wish you had. Enter too fast, and you'll be going backwards right now. When the maneuver is done correctly, the car will U-turn in its own length. Practice on a big, wide, friendly space first.

1. Start of turn. Rear wheels are locked by emergency brake. Steering wheel is at hard left. If you lock first, then turn, the vehicle will turn in a narrower space. We used Mac's Miata for the sequence because it's small and photogenic, but this can be done in virtually any vehicle. Secret Service agents practice it in big limos and Suburbans.

2. Rear wheels slide, spinning car over 90 degrees in its own length. Mac has already straightened the steering wheel of the agile Miata.

3. As tail comes around, he releases brake, shifts car into first (manual transmission). Mac has corrected for rear wheel skid in an effort to catch it before car exceeds 180 degrees.

4. As tail comes on around, steering is far to right.

5. Tail is around. Mac is letting wheel self-center and applying throttle. Some cars self-center better than others. Do what's necessary.

6. Apply throttle and drive away in opposite direction.

South. If they're worrying about it now, they have their priorities wrong. This maneuver enables you to change directions 180 degrees without stopping, within the width of a two-lane road. It is useful in evading pursuers or avoiding roadblocks. When I was practicing this, I could do this on a one-lane dirt road with trees on both sides. I wasn't running moonshine (born too late). I found it useful on rallies, and it was a lot of fun.

It is best done with a car having an automatic transmission and a hand emergency brake, but I learned it on a stick-shift car, so it can be done. It just uses more hands. A stick shift and a foot-operated emergency brake with a hand-operated release might make you run out of hands. If you have a foot-operated emergency brake you will find it easier to do if you deactivate the ratchet mechanism of the emergency brake. In other words, pushing the foot down should activate the emergency brake, and letting it up should release it. I've used pieces of wood that, when wedged under the emergency brake release, will cause it to stay permanently released. With other cars a little duct tape can solve the problem. But it means you have to set the car up for bootlegger hairpins ahead of time. With a handbrake, you don't have to do anything, but if the push-button ratchet release is balky, you can unscrew it or tape the button down depending on the design, making it a flyoff handbrake.

And be sure your car will do it. Back in the late '50s there was an autocross, then called a gymkhana. A bunch of MGs were running, and the course layout appeared to be perfect for a handbrake hairpin. The cars were to accelerate from one turn, do a 180-degree turn around a pylon, then run back to the previous turn and retrace the route in reverse. After one driver tried using the handbrake to cause the car to skid 180 degrees, everyone tried it. (By the way, this isn't the quickest way on the autocross track. We set up a timer one day and practiced all the basic autocross situations, starts, finishes, various kinds of turns. The U-turn around a pylon was best done as a constant radius turn.)

But one contestant had a BMW Isetta, a little buglike car with the door in front and fairly narrow track in the back. He watched all of the MG-TCs, TDs, and MG-TFs use their handbrakes and tried it himself. He went screaming up to the pylon, turned the wheel, declutched, and pulled on the handbrake . . . and the car tipped over on its side.

Here's how to do the bootlegger hairpin:

1. Slow to 25–35 mph.
2. Take your foot off the gas. Grab the steering wheel at the 9-10 o'clock position with the left hand and spin it to the 3-4 o'clock position while *simultaneously* applying the emergency brake *hard*. Depress the clutch.
3. When the car spins 90 to 100 degrees, release the emergency brake,

The Gizmo, a piece of wood carved to fit in the slots to hold the emergency brake release in the "release" position for ease of doing bootlegger hairpins. This one is attached so it hangs below the brake release when not in use and can be put into place as needed. It should be kept in place and removed only when using the brake as a parking brake.

floor the throttle, release the clutch, and straighten the steering wheel. With a responsive car you'll have to countersteer to prevent its spinning out completely.

4. Accelerate at full throttle. If you're being chased, the goblin is close, and it's dark, it's a good idea to hit the bright lights at this point. (See Useful Gadgets chapter.)

Practice

First, inflate your tires to 40 psi. If you have hubcaps, leave them at home. For that matter, leave everything in the car that is loose at home. Don't practice on a tree-lined one-lane road, but a wide-open parking lot. I found it easier to learn on sand and gravel because it wasn't as hard on the tires. Expect to use up a set of front tires if you do this much on pavement. It is *very* hard on front tires. You cannot do it at reduced speed, and you cannot do it and be gentle. If you're not going fast enough, the car won't skid. If you don't jam on the emergency brake, the car won't skid. If you don't whip the wheel quickly and far enough, you won't complete the maneuver. If you try it too fast, the car will go backward. If you should do this in a real live chase situation, floor the throttle in first, spinning the tires. When they get enough traction, you will shoot ahead.

Check transmission fluid levels and oil levels before and after practicing.

Please be aware that owners of parking lots frown on people using their lots for practicing wild evasive maneuvers. Getting permission is usually impossible, so practicing in short sessions is advised.

I remember teaching a young woman how to do handbrake hairpins once in the '70s on a deserted gravel parking lot. Gravel makes it easier on the tires. She had just about learned it when someone with a keen sense of his own importance drove up demanding to know what we were doing. I explained that we were plotting the chase scene of an upcoming Burt Reynolds movie, that Burt would be crossing the bridge down the street at full throttle and be diverted into the parking lot by a roadblock, where he would do a bootlegger hairpin and escape. The woman with me was the stunt double for the female lead (and looked like she could play the female lead, which distracted him nicely). We would, of course, be paying for the use of the parking lot.

He liked that idea and gave us his name and phone number for further coordination. I suppose when Burt and Lonnie broke up he figured out there wouldn't be a *Smoky and the Bandit Go to Texas*.

Certain SAABs have the handbrake work the front wheels. Do not expect to do a hand-brake hairpin in one of those. (How that got past Eric Carlson I'll never know.)

The Moonshiner's Turn

The Moonshiner's Turn or reverse 180 degrees is another useful maneuver credited to the former traffickers in untaxed adult beverages. This allows you to change directions 180 degrees within the confines of a two-lane road while going backward. This is particularly useful at roadblocks.

1. Accelerate in reverse to 20–30 mph (you'll have to estimate). The speedometer doesn't work in reverse, and you can't see it while going backward, anyway.

2. Take your foot off the gas, spin the steering wheel hard left as fast as you can. The left hand at 3-5 o'clock spinning left to 9-10 o'clock works on this, too.

3. When the car reaches 90 degrees, shift to first (low, etc., in automatic transmission cars), stand on the throttle, and straighten the steering wheel. Done properly, the car never stops, but changes direction of travel. A stopped car is a sitting target.

4. Exit the area. Keep low. If they're shooting at you, the trunk and back seat offer some protection.

Most roadblocks at night use high-intensity spotlights or headlights aimed at you. This allows you to look away from them because you'll be wanting to look behind you while you're backing up.

When practicing this, do note that shifting to first or drive while going backward in reverse is one of the hardest things you can do to an automatic transmission. Also note that a car going in reverse at 20–30 mph, because the turning wheels are in the back, isn't particularly stable or easy to control. So practice should be done in a large, unobstructed parking lot. The diagrams show doing the turn to the left because normally there's more room to the left. The photos show Mad Mac doing them to the right because that's the way he wanted to

The Moonshiner's Turn

Accelerate in reverse to 20–30 mph (position 1). Get off the throttle and crank the steering wheel to the left as fast as you can. (Grip at 3 o'clock with left hand like bootlegger hairpin and move wheel as far as you can.) To get from position 2 to position 3, shift into first, floor the accelerator, turn the wheel hard right, and accelerate at flank.

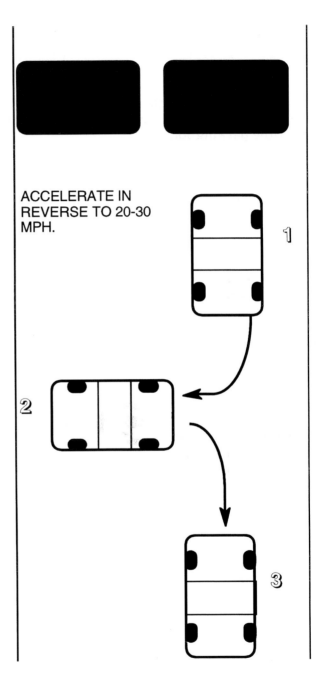

ACCELERATE IN REVERSE TO 20-30 MPH.

1. Mac approaches the road block. Once the driver realizes it's an ambush, he stops as hard and fast as he can. This makes the people manning the roadblock think he's stopping for them.

2. Mac shifts into reverse and accelerates at flank. If someone is shooting or likely to, get as low as you can in the car.

3. Mac gets up a good head of steam and looks in the direction he intends to turn. Mac turns to the right. I turn to the left, because there's usually more room to the left since we drive on the right side of the road.

4. Mac spins the wheel hard right and brakes . . .

5. . . . . shifts to first while still going backwards, and floors the throttle, changing momentum from backwards to forwards as quickly as possible so as not to present a stationary target. This maneuver can be done without ever stopping the car.

6. Now with momentum going forward, Mac accelerates away from the danger zone in the direction from which he came.

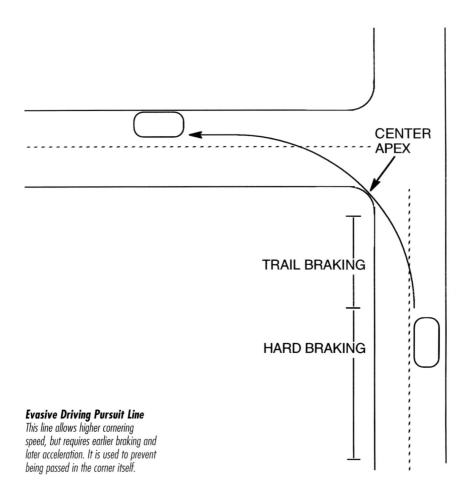

CENTER
APEX

TRAIL BRAKING

HARD BRAKING

Evasive Driving Pursuit Line
This line allows higher cornering
speed, but requires earlier braking and
later acceleration. It is used to prevent
being passed in the corner itself.

do them. As long as you get away, it doesn't matter, of course.

One proponent of these maneuvers recommends practicing them in cars belonging to Hertz, Avis, and other agencies. Personally, I would consider this rental-car abuse and would never recommend such a thing.

No Passing Lines

Pursuit line: This is the line to use if the road is clear and your pursuer is in danger of passing you. In the example given, obviously it would only work if your visibility is such that you can see that there is no traffic approaching the intersection. It uses all of the road, and it results in the highest cornering speed through the turn, making it less likely that you will be passed during the turn. Braking will have to be a car length or two earlier than the racing line, and because of the cornering arc, you won't be able to put down maximum power as early. If you watch road races, you will note this line being used by drivers who are trying to avoid being passed.

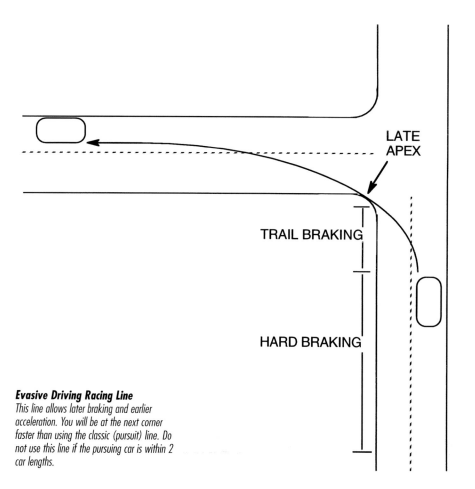

LATE
APEX

TRAIL BRAKING

HARD BRAKING

Evasive Driving Racing Line
This line allows later braking and earlier acceleration. You will be at the next corner faster than using the classic (pursuit) line. Do not use this line if the pursuing car is within 2 car lengths.

This is your goal, too. The difference here is your life may depend on not being passed. A passenger in a car passing you can shoot you, or the driver can run you off the road. Don't worry, we'll teach you how to run *him* off the road.

Racing line: This is the line you would use on a racetrack for fastest lap times. It gives the fastest time for the entire corner, but the cornering speed at apex is a little lower than with the pursuit line. You can brake later and get on the accelerator a little quicker, but don't use it if the guy is right on your tail, as he might be able to pass you. (We'll talk about what to do about that under Contact Sports.)

Traffic line: This shows a variation to handle traffic—in this case, a car stopped at a stop sign or traffic light at the intersection. You can't use the whole road, but you use all you can of it, leaving room for the stopped car. If your pursuer hits the stopped car and ends the pursuit, well, that's bad for the poor guy at the intersection, but at least it ends the pursuit.

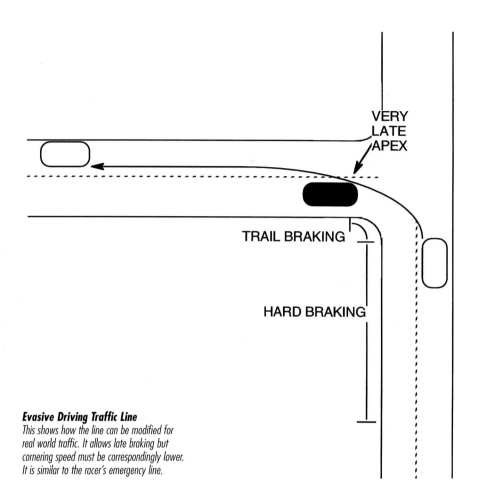

VERY
LATE
APEX

TRAIL BRAKING

HARD BRAKING

Evasive Driving Traffic Line
This shows how the line can be modified for real world traffic. It allows late braking but cornering speed must be correspondingly lower. It is similar to the racer's emergency line.

In actual chase situations the likelihood of racetrack precision is unlikely. You will be making snap decisions based on sight reading the approaching corner or intersection. Conservative, intelligent fast driving will usually win because your pursuer is unlikely to be well trained in pursuit.

Contact Sports

Sometimes your pursuer will catch you. Sometimes you will confront roadblocks. All is not lost even if those things occur. With the combat mindset, good tactics, and mastery of your weapon, the vehicle, you can still escape. But it might be time to use the vehicle as a weapon, not just an escape tool.

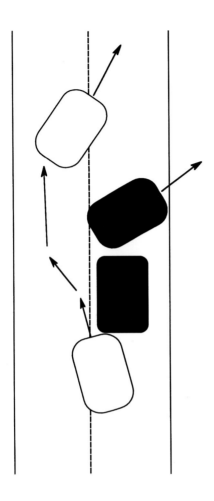

To knock a vehicle off the road, hit it with the bumper of your car at a 15- to 25-degree angle. You should be going 10 to 20 mph faster than he is. If contact speed exceeds 13 mph (3 G's), expect the airbag(s) to go off.

Where to hit someone to knock him off the road and stay on it yourself

If your attacker does pass you, this might be opportunity knocking. It's pretty easy for the car behind to knock the car in front off the road. Having had it done to me on racetracks, I can attest to this.

One method involves going 10–20 mph faster than the car in front, and hitting the left corner of his rear bumper with the right corner of yours. Hit, don't push. With modern cars a hit within 30 degrees of frontal exceeding 3 Gs will set off your air bag(s), except for Mercedes-Benz, which require a 4 G deceleration to fire the air bag if your seat belt is fastened. A bag firing does not disable your car, so ignore it. The bag will be deflated in your lap in less than a second after it is fired. If you don't let it startle you, you can continue to drive. The bag will get very hot in your lap.

93

In this situation, pull along side of other vehicle's rear and crash into the rear, behind the rear wheels, in front of his rear bumper. This will cause him to spin across the road. Upon contact, brake and countersteer to break contact.

After impact the opposition's vehicle will go sliding sideways until his tires regain traction. When this happens, his car will go the direction it is pointing, which should be off the road.

The second method involves pulling up beside, or, if the goblin has started to pass you in an effort to run you off the road, to brake until your front bumper is between the rear wheel and the rear bumper, then jerk the steering wheel to the right until you hit him smartly. He will spin in front of you. Be prepared to brake and countersteer immediately to break contact. He should spin off the road to the left without further contact with you.

This shouldn't set off the air bag. Air bags won't normally go off at an angled hit like this, and, from your standpoint, this isn't as hard a hit as the previous technique, thus a better technique to use in an air bag-equipped car.

The center of your vehicle should be pressing against the front bumper of the target car.

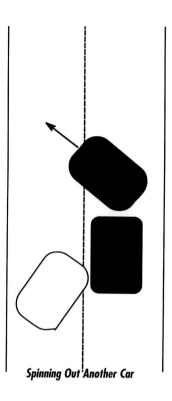

Spinning Out Another Car

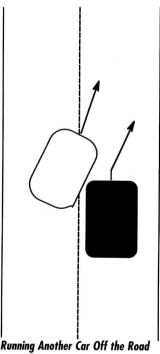

Running Another Car Off the Road

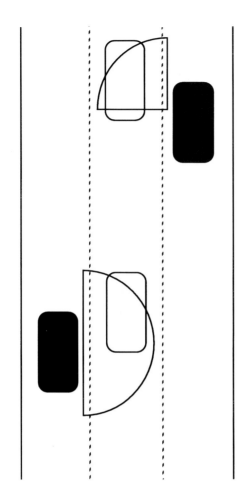

Running another car off the road

This might be what the black car in the previous illustration was doing to you. Be careful, as he can turn the tables on you if he's good and spin you off the road. You must be ahead of the other vehicle, with the center of your vehicle pressing against the front of his vehicle. By doing this, you are using your total body weight against only a small portion of the other vehicle. A small car can force a much larger car off the road.

If someone tries this on you, if you brake hard and get your front bumper behind his rear wheel arch, you can spin him off the road using the previous technique.

Danger Zones

Don't let someone stay in your blind spot for any length of time. A common method of killing that has migrated from Central America to urban gangs in the United States is to pull alongside a victim's car and start shooting, using a lot of rounds, full automatic fire if possible, or 20–30 rounds of quick semi-automatic fire (which is more accurate anyway).

Don't wait for the attack to happen. Slam on the brakes, let the attacker go, and if the attack is starting, either turn off the road after you've braked, or do a bootlegger's hairpin to exit the area.

95

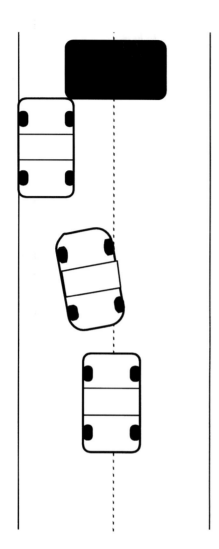

The Single Car Roadblock
Slow almost to a halt, then first gear and floor the throttle. First choice is between rear wheel and rear bumper. Second choice is between front wheel and front bumper. Keep accelerator floored through impact. Keep going, even if the car is badly damaged.

Motorcycles are used in Central American shootings, even in heavy traffic. The shooter is the passenger on the motorcycle. The driver pulls up beside an unsuspecting car and the passenger sprays the car with automatic weapons fire, then they speed away through the heavy traffic. If the attacker is a motorcyclist, simply turn into him, knocking him off the road, neutralizing the threat. In this case size does count.

Roadblocks

Roadblock attacks aren't yet a problem in the United States, but they are in Central America, and it won't be long before the gangs here start escalating to this. In Houston gangs have been doing their "initiation" killings by simply finding someone at a roadside phone booth and shooting him, usually with no motive. They've shot other gang members in drive-by and car-to-car shootings as described above. Roadblocks are possibly next, so it's good to know how to defeat them.

Single-Vehicle Roadblocks

If a single vehicle is sitting across the road in a roadblock with armed or otherwise dangerous men manning it, slow down as if you are going to stop for it. This will give the goblins a false sense of security.

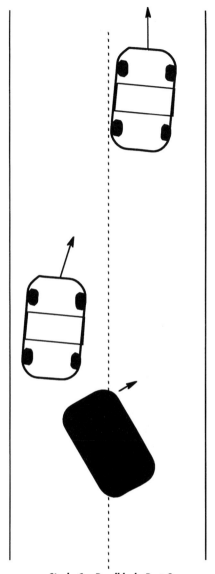

Single Car Roadblock, Part 2

Put the vehicle into low gear and suddenly go to full throttle. If it is night, turn on all of your lights if they aren't on already.

Aim for, in order of preference: 1) The rear fender area between the rear wheel and the bumper, or 2) The front fender in front of the front wheel. One end or another might be against a curb or wall, forcing you to ram the other.

Hit at an angle and keep the accelerator floored through the collision. You should hit the vehicle between 15 and 30 mph. Expect the air bag(s) to deploy. (They may not. Hitting a car's fender isn't the same as hitting a concrete bridge abutment. The car will give. Also you're only hitting with one corner of your car.)

Keep going, even if your car is badly damaged. You must get out of the area at all costs.

The Two-Vehicle Roadblock

This is serious bad news, and ramming must be considered the least attractive alternative. The Bootlegger's Hairpin and the Moonshiner's Turn must be considered first, of course. Unless someone is also chasing you, ramming through a two-vehicle roadblock is one of those things you just do not want to do. Even if someone is chasing you, one of the evasive maneuvers is preferable. Anyone doing a two-vehicle roadblock

The Two Vehicle Roadblock

This is the last ditch maneuver of all last ditch maneuvers. Slow almost to a stop. Put car into first gear. Floor the throttle. Contact speed should be 20–30 mph. Keep throttle floored through the collision. Keep low in the car. Keep going at all cost.

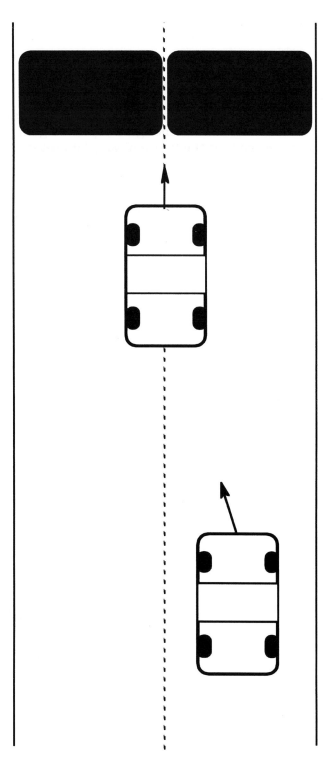

will have sufficient people manning it that it is likely you will be driving through a gauntlet of gunfire, and ramming two vehicles will very likely make yours undrivable quite soon. I've included instructions for ramming it, but the likelihood that I would employ the ram is somewhere between slim and none.

Slow almost to a complete stop and put the car into low gear.

Hit full throttle far enough away to be going between 20 and 30 mph when you hit the two vehicles. Aim between them and keep the throttle floored through the collision. Expect the air bag(s) to deploy.

After breaking through, keep going as fast as you can. It is likely your vehicle will become undrivable soon.

It goes without saying, but I'll say it anyway, since you're only running a roadblock in a life-or-death situation, it is kosher to run over any of your attackers who don't get out of the way.

Keep low in the vehicle. They will be shooting at you.

High Speeds

Use high speed carefully and sparingly. Going through city streets at high speeds usually results in a crash, and you cannot afford to crash. On the open road, if you have a faster car and are comfortable with high speeds, go for it.

The Left Side

Try to keep a pursuer from pulling up beside you. He can either shoot you or run you off the road. Drive to the left. Swerve in front of him.

Jumping Curbs

If you must jump a curb, do so at an angle, 45 degrees and less than 45 mph. Yes, it might damage your car. The trick is to avoid blowing tires and breaking wheels. Jumping a curb is preferable to ramming a roadblock, whether it is one lane or two.

Never Give Up

If you are unconscious or dead you may give up. If you are taken by the goblins nothing good will happen, and statistically fighting back works better than giving in. Fighting back with skill works even better. Fighting back with skill, cunning, and ruthlessness works best of all.

Training

Several of the driving schools listed in the High-Performance Driving chapter teach special courses in Anti-Terrorist, Anti-Kidnapping Driving. First, I would take a high-performance course, then I would take the Anti-Terrorist, Anti-Kidnapping course. The Bob Bondurant School spends enough time on basic high-performance driving that it will suffice if your attitude is good. When I was taking the three-day

High Performance Course in 1976, two guys were taking the Anti-Terrorist, Anti-Kidnap course. They were sent by their employers, and neither would tell who his employer was. Both were used to driving big cars and chauffeuring VIPs. One took to the course quickly and did well. The other would not push the car hard enough. He was used to driving gently and was reluctant to change. Evasive driving is not gentle. You may have to sacrifice the car to save your life.

The point is that the Bob Bondurant School instructors can teach you the techniques needed to survive. They cannot provide the combat mindset. Currently the Bondurant school has a separate division for anti-kidnap, anti-terrorist driving, corporate chauffeurs, etc. They have several different courses.

CHAPTER SEVEN

KIDNAPPING AND CARJACKING

Incident 10

In the eighties, Aldo Moro, the Italian Prime Minister, was kidnapped by terrorists and eventually found in the trunk of a car, his body riddled with small-caliber bullets from a Czech machine pistol.

Incident 11

Recently a young, attractive woman was kidnapped at gunpoint from a shopping center parking lot. She was placed in the passenger's seat of a pickup truck. She jumped out of the vehicle at 70 mph on a busy freeway and escaped. She survived this and testified against her kidnapper in court. He was convicted and sentenced to 60 years. The kidnapper is also the main suspect in the disappearance and murder of two young girls in the area, one 12, one a teenager. He had been previously convicted of similar crimes in another state.

Incident 12

A Lexus owner was bumped at a stop sign. He angrily jumped out of the car to confront the driver. The driver and passenger got out of the car, and the Lexus owner, distracted by the driver, didn't notice the passenger until he felt the gun against the side of his head. They took his car. He survived.

Incident 13

A gas station had arranged for self-service after hours, using credit cards. The station was totally unattended. Randy pulled in, inserted his credit card, and began to get gas when he noticed the pickup truck on the other side wasn't getting gas. Two males got out of the truck. One engaged Randy in conversation, saying they had run out of gas and were out of money. The other began to try to work his way around behind Randy. Randy carried a legally concealed pistol and put his hand on it. This caused the carjackers to get back in their truck and drive off looking for easier prey.

Incident 14

A woman was getting gas at a self-service station. A recently released parolee demanded her keys. She gave them to him. He shot and killed her and took the car. The car was a cheap, common Japanese sedan.

Incident 15

A woman loaded down with packages approached her car at a mall. A man attacked her and demanded her keys. She managed to push the "panic" button on her alarm, and the noise scared him away. Police caught him soon after. He was wanted for rape and murder in another state.

Incident 16

A young woman was waiting in a drive-through line at a fast food restaurant. A young man shot her and dragged her body out of the blood-soaked car and drove away. At his trial he admitted he did it. He had run out of gas in the getaway car from a convenience store robbery. He had killed her to get a car with a tank of gas.

Incident 17

A young mother, as she started to get into her car in a parking lot, was thrown to the ground by an attacker, who took the car and drove off. Her baby was strapped into the back seat, so she tried to hang onto the car to rescue the child. Her attackers brushed the car against a guardrail to dislodge her, killing her. Later, they threw the baby, car seat and all, out on the median of the freeway. The child survived because of the baby seat.

Incident 18

A woman walking to her car at a mall noted an old woman in distress, leaning against a car. She asked if the old woman needed help. She said yes, she was sick. The woman had the presence of mind to say, "I'll get a security guard" and leave. She returned with the security guard. The woman was gone. A search started, and the old woman was found, hiding in a truck. The "old woman" was a man in women's clothes, with a small ax taped to his chest.

Avoiding Carjacking

1. Remember, situational awareness is the key. Condition Yellow. It is very difficult to carjack a moving vehicle. The danger comes when you're stopped. You should have a plan for contingencies when you stop. You should know what you're going to do. It's much easier for a fear/adrenaline shocked brain to say, "A, B, and C have happened, therefore I do D," than it is to figure out a plan on the spot.

2. Leave space between your car and the one in front of you at traffic lights and stop signs so you can drive around that car in a quick

escape. This is something you need to practice, using, for example, your spouse's car in a parking lot. Pull up behind it. How close can you get and still get around it? Learn that distance. Use it every day, all of the time. If in doubt, leave a little extra room. Half a car length usually works. Usually if you can see its rear tires, you can steer around it. Then you can't be boxed in.

3. If someone approaches that you don't know, leave now. If you see someone approaching with a weapon, try to get away now, making as much noise as possible. Stand on the horn, activate the flashers as you try to get away. *Now* is the time to get away. Goblins don't go to shooting schools. At 20 feet away, they're poor shots. At 10 feet, they're better. If the gun's touching the window glass, they can't miss. Run *now* while you have range on your side. (Attend a shooting school if you have to learn how to shoot; now is also the time to shoot if you need to. To a trained shooter someone 20 feet away is an easy target, while the goblin shooting or threatening to shoot you will probably miss.)

4. If the person is already holding the weapon *on* you when you realize you have a problem, don't resist at this point. Your car is not worth your life; it won't die for you. Don't die for your car. At this point your goal is to survive. Use conciliatory words, as few as possible, and *give him the keys*. If you're out of the car when you have to give him the keys, drop them "accidentally" and run. He wants the keys; he doesn't want to shoot you. If he's so whacked out on drugs that he shoots you, he would have anyway. Your mistake was letting him get the drop on you.

5. *Do not* reach for your purse or anything else in the car. The attacker might think you are reaching for a gun and shoot you. Your purse won't die for you; don't die for it.

6. If your child is in the car and you are forced out and cannot grab the child, yell immediately, "There's a baby in the car!" Carjackers are not rocket scientists. They're dumb, lazy, heartless goblins. But if they have any snap at all, they know that the cops will move heaven and earth to find a kidnapped baby, where a stolen car is no big deal. Additionally, the penalty when they're caught just went up. Do be aware that the carjacker is most likely on drugs, and his reaction might not be reasonable. But if he gets away with the child, the odds are he'll throw the child out when he realizes it, and children have been killed that way. If he lets you take the child now, everyone is better off. Don't get killed to save the child. It won't save the child, and if you're alive, you can tell the cops there's a child in the car. You'll know your license plate and a good description of the car, and they *will* move heaven and earth to find him.

7. Check your rearview mirror often to see if anyone is following you. Use the techniques of Chapter Six to determine if the driver behind you is, call the police, and head for one of the places mentioned: a police substation, a fire station, a hospital emergency room, etc. Turn on your emergency flashers and honk the horn. If your alarm has a panic button that will set it off, push it now. This will bring enough attention to you to run off 99 percent of carjackers and kidnappers.

8. *Exercise to prevent being followed home* (repeated from Chapter Six for emphasis):
Find a spot on your route where you turn right. As you approach that spot, notice who is behind you. If someone follows you through that turn who doesn't look particularly righteous, make another right turn at the next intersection that doesn't take you into a dead end. If he's still there, make one more. If he's still there, see the entry immediately above.

9. Carry a cellular phone. Put 911 into the speed dial or pre-dial it. Motorolas will automatically dial 911 if you hold button #1. Under severe stress and adrenaline overload, with shaking fingers, this is about all you can do.

10. If someone hits your car, especially from the rear, see if the passenger is getting out as well as the driver. If so, do not stop. Run *away*! Note the license plate if you can. Serious goblins often don't have front plates or cover them with mud. Drive with your flashers on to the nearest police station or flag down a police car or dial 911 on your car phone. Do not get out of the car and confront them. Most men will immediately jump out of the car to check the damage. Thus distracted, they are easy prey. If it was a legitimate accident, tell them to follow you to a gas station or convenience store, etc., to exchange information. Your excuse is to get the cars off the main road. In reality, you want witnesses around so they won't try anything. If they refuse, drive away at flank. If you keep a preprinted card with your insurance information on it, you can slide that out the window to give the other driver in case of a real accident.
People allow themselves to get carjacked because they're concentrating on making sure the other party's insurance pays for the accident. Before you concern yourself with that, make sure it *is* an accident and not a felony in progress.
A few years back a woman ran from a carjacking rear-ender, and when she reported to the police, they arrested her for leaving the scene of the accident! This was settled in court where a jury acquitted her, but by now the police in most major cities have learned, though it's not wise to ever overestimate the intelligence of traffic cops. I believe I would start my conversation with the nice officer by saying I had just run away

from an attempted carjacking. He can find out that you were struck from behind during the conversation. "Officer, I just ran away from an attempted carjacking. The car involved was a white Chevrolet Suburban, front license plate started with PJ, and then the rest was obscured. The occupants were three large white males wearing baseball caps. It occurred at the corner of Sixth and Olive." Now, he has enough information to start asking questions. Now don't tell him anything he doesn't ask for. If, instead, you tried to describe the mechanics of how you were rear-ended first, he might think you left the scene of an accident.

11. Avoiding double teaming. A car behind you knocks you into the one in front of you, and they're both in on it. Now you're blocked. See point 1 above. If this occurs anyway, before they can get out of the car with guns, ram back and forth until you can run away.

I saw the condition of a big BMW that had been double-teamed. The driver had escaped, but the car was totaled by the repeated battering of both ends. This is acceptable. Your car is insured; you can replace it. You can't replace your head after it's blown off.

12. Have your keys in hand before you walk outside to your car *and look around when leaving buildings. Make sure your path is clear to the car.* Keep your car keys separate from your house keys. This is important. If someone does get your car, they'll have your address from your registration, insurance card, and owner's manual/warranty book, unless you register your cars to your business address (which is not a bad idea). If they also have your keys, you'll have to change the locks on your house, and the thief might get there before you can do that.

13. Don't overburden yourself with packages. Ask a store employee to help carry some or make multiple trips. When shopping, take a friend if possible or bring the car to the loading area in front of the store and have a store employee bring the packages out.

14. Peer quickly through windows to make sure no one is hiding in your car. If it's clear, get in immediately; don't dawdle outside. I don't like privacy glass, and this is one reason. A smart thief (admittedly a rarity) can get into the car and hide. A remote that, when you unlock the driver's door, turns on the interior lights while you get in, is a good idea. Do note I said "when you unlock the driver's door." The best locking systems now have a system by which you can unlock just the driver's door and possibly the gas cap door, not the whole car. And beware of the Cadillacs with a system that locks the car when you put it into drive but unlocks it when you put it into park. A thief waiting only has to hear you put it into park to know he can now open the door. This, by the way, can be deactivated by dealers.

15. Consider a good, comprehensive security system with remote and panic like the Alpine SEC8058 (as of summer 1997, the state of the art) so you can set off the alarm at will. High-line cars are coming with increasingly more sophisticated alarms and anti-theft keys, with the Mercedes-Benz "Smart Key" being perhaps the state of the art. All electronic, the key is copy proof, has anti-cloning coding in the radio remote, and has a built-in panic button. For the purpose of preventing carjacking, motion detectors and shock sensors aren't necessary. They help in preventing vandalization of the car, but anyone trying to steal the car must open a door, so just door sensors are enough for the alarm. If it uses a radio remote, anti-cloning coding is a must. Otherwise you might find someone in your car when you return to it. By anti-cloning I mean a rolling code so that someone with a code capture box can't sit in the parking lot, and when you lock the car, capture your remote's frequency and code, play it back, and unlock the car. Remotes using anti-cloning send two numerical codes which total a secret number. Each time the remote is used, it sends different codes. They always add up to the same number, but a code capture box can't use them and play them back. The receiver will only accept a *different* set of figures adding up to the same number.

16. Keep windows rolled up when you park. Don't leave a small crack. With a small crack, a thief can open the door using appropriate tools, which I won't go into here for fear of training car thieves. Most of them get quite enough training on the street and in prison.

17. Many cars can be opened with a "slimjim," a device for opening doors without a key, useful to tow truck drivers. Alarms defeat that.

18. Always, always lock your car (basic, but true).

19. Keep a flashlight in your car in case it breaks down after dark. Since, as the bumper sticker says, "A flashlight is a case for dead batteries," replace them on time-change days, in the spring and fall when you go on and off daylight-saving time. I recommend the small lithium-battery flashlight such as the Sure-Fire series. They're available in 1-, 2-, and 3-battery models, and in combat light models with ridges for use in the weak hand of a two-handed hold of a pistol. The 3-volt, 1-battery unit is only 3.5 inches long, weighs 4.0 ounces, and provides 60 minutes of run time. The 6-volt, 2-battery units are 4.9 inches long, weigh 5.0 ounces and provide 75 minutes of run time. The 9-volt, 3-battery unit provides 105 minutes of run time. These lights give good, clear light without dark spots or rings. These lights are small enough to fit into the glovebox, side pocket, or console. Big 3 and 4 D-cell Mag lights and the like become lethal missiles in a crash if lying loose in the back seat.

20. Avoid the curbside lane when driving in *heavy* traffic. Fast operators can break a car window, unlock the door, and be inside within seconds. This applies to the median-side lane in heavy-enough traffic. I do know of an acquaintance whose car was attacked by someone from the median who ripped open his convertible top with a pick, just missing the driver's head. This was accompanied by the command, "Give me your keys and get out!" The driver, while the pick was stuck in the convertible top, floored the throttle, climbing the median curb, and dragging the goblin with him until he let go of the pick. Traffic opened up enough for him to outrun the goblin. Two days later the driver enrolled in training for a concealed handgun license and now carries one all of the time.

In *light* traffic stay out of the middle lane. Either the left or the right lane is safer. Four cars can box you in the middle lane.

21. The right front seat is the best place for a child seat for anti-carjacking because the carjacker can see it, but the least safe in a crash. (If you have two air bags, it must go in the rear.) (Note, however, that 1998 and later Mercedes-Benzes have BabySmart™, which uses Mercedes-Benz infant, toddler, or child booster seats, which disable the air bag while the child seat is in place, making the right front seat safe again for children. Cars with air bag cut-off switches for the passenger seat are also safe for infants and small children if the airbag is switched off.)

22. Keep your car in good repair. Never allow the fuel gauge to fall below a quarter tank. A major police force has been estimated that a woman in a broken down car's odds of being attacked increase to a near 100 percent after half an hour.

23. Keep your house key with you when you valet park.

24. If you pay at a store with cash, put it away before you leave the register, no matter how long the line behind you.

25. Your garage is a good place for muggers:
Drive into your garage front-first so your headlights illuminate the total area. Odds are there is a place on one side or the other that is in shadow, where a goblin could hide and then jump you as you come out of the car.

Automatic garage door openers help. Open the garage at the last minute, and close it as soon as your car's inside.

If your garage door opener is a few years old, consider upgrading it to a rolling code model similar in concept to the alarms mentioned in point 15 above. Kits are available at stores that sell garage door openers and in Griot's Garage mail-order catalog, 1-800-345-5789. Older garage door openers used one frequency and one code set by opening the unit and flipping some of several little switches in an effort to come up with an unique code. A TV station near me took a transmitter with the switches in the default setting as they left the factory and opened an awful lot of garage doors. I'm sure this gave as many thieves ideas as it did owners. If you can't afford to upgrade to a rolling code, do change the code in your unit if it's at the default code.

Consider adding bump-stops so you can close the door as soon as you feel you're touching one.

Check out your garage for security. Think like a mugger. If there are bushes or shrubs a mugger can hide in, take them down. Ideally, as you approach, your lights should illuminate enough area to prevent a carjacker or kidnapper from hiding. If there are places he can hide, do something about them.

(Normally, I carry a small .45, which I am lawfully licensed to do in Texas. When in the car I usually keep it in a holster in the driver's side door pocket. When I get out of the car at the house, I pick up the pistol, then open the door, not holstering it until I'm clear. This would make it very difficult for a goblin to surprise me. I find it impossible to remain in Condition White while a pistol is in my hand.)

26. Walking to and from your car:

Walk with a purse held close to your body, away from the flow of traffic.

Be alert and walk with confidence.

Scan the parking lot.

Follow your instincts. If something looks wrong, it probably is. Go back into the building, and get help of whatever sort is available.

One problem of working people is we enter and leave the parking lot at work at the same time every day. We also leave the house and return at approximately the same time every day. If you can't vary your schedule, remember that you're vulnerable there. The bad guys know when you'll be there. It's imperative that you not be in Condition White at these points. I know you do this every day, but that's the point. They do, too, and they figure you'll be most vulnerable then.

Pepper spray is better than Mace or the other self-defense sprays. Remember that if fired upwind, it can come back and incapacitate you, too. Some states require training and certification to carry pepper spray. If that isn't required or available, learn completely the instructions that come with it. Don't leave a unit in a hot car all summer. Eventually it might blow up in the heat, putting pepper spray all over the inside of the car. (Trust me on this. A can of Mace did in my car once, and it wasn't pleasant.)

The stun gun, a battery-powered electrical device that transmits enough shock to incapacitate most people, does not work on everyone, and they all require solid contact with the upper body of the target person. Used properly, stun guns will put him down for a couple of minutes, long enough to let you escape. But there are too many documented cases of felons deflecting the gun or just absorbing it without being incapacitated. Also law suits have resulted from the use of stun guns by police officers. Additionally, the stun guns available to civilians require contact with the attacker. If you can touch him, he can touch you, and if he's bigger and stronger than you, he'll take it away from you and turn it on you.

In researching this I called a buddy on the local SWAT team. The SWAT team uses a Taser gun, which operates on the same concept of electrical shock, but shoots the contacts to the target, so it can be used from a few feet away. The Taser failed 22 out of 26 times in their use, and they've had to try other means. He recommended pepper spray, but with all of the reservations I mentioned.

27. Don't leave your purse or wallet in plain view on the seat next to you when driving. Put it under the passenger seat where it doesn't show from the outside.

28. *Avoiding getting carjacked at a gas station:* Condition Yellow is the key. Instead of putting all of your concentration into getting gas, keep your eyes up and look around. When you first pull in, note every other car at the station. Note the attendant in the little glass booth. Pick a pump that allows you to maintain eye contact with him. He can't be counted on to help in a carjacking, but thieves will generally pick a spot without witnesses. If the only open pump is around back, out of sight from the road and the attendant, don't take it. Wait or go to another station.

Before you get out of the car, have your credit card accessible. Take it out of your wallet and put it in a pocket. I choose stations that allow credit card payment at the pump for both convenience and safety. Not going into the convenience store when I don't need to keeps me out of one place in harm's way. If anyone around is suspicious, get back into your car and go to another station. When getting out, unlock only the driver's door, if you can. If you have a remote you can relock the car when you get out, preventing anyone from climbing in the other side. If all is clear, while inserting the credit card and filling the tank, look around. You don't have to watch the gas pump unless you're paying cash and trying to stop filling at an even number. This gives the advantage to credit cards. Keep looking around as you replace the pump and get your receipt. If you have to go to the window to pay, make sure the car is locked completely, using your remote.

When you get back into the car, lock the doors immediately. If you record fuel mileage, for a minute or so you have to have your concentration inside the car. This is a vulnerable point. If anyone around is suspicious, leave the station and record fuel mileage half a mile down the road, if necessary.

If there are two of you in the car, the armed one should watch the other fill the tank.

29. ATM machines: The same basic rules apply. Stay in Condition Yellow. Be suspicious. If anyone is hanging around suspiciously, leave. If there are two of you, the armed one should stand guard over the one doing the transaction. Needless to say, take all receipts and paperwork with you. If the ATM machine is enclosed, your money should be in your pocket or purse before leaving the enclosure.

30. Most important, follow your instincts and get out of any suspicious situations immediately. This sounds like common sense, but it is surprising how many people are afraid to act because they don't want to be embarrassed.

31. No one was ever carjacked in Condition Yellow. If you're alert, you can avoid carjacking. You have a marvelous 3,000-pound weapon and your brain, the best weapon of all.

How Much of a Kidnap Target Are You?

Do remember that almost everyone is something of a kidnap target. In some kidnappings, the victims were just targets of opportunity. A bank robber needed a hostage. A serial rapist saw a woman in Condition White. Big, strong men driving cheap pickup trucks have been kidnapped as hostages on the spur of the moment by desperate men with guns. But, of course, some people are serious kidnap targets for planned kidnappings aimed at them personally.

Age: Older people are easier to kidnap. Of course, the children of wealthy people are easy to kidnap and are serious kidnap targets. Appearance counts. How tough do you look? A frail person looks easier to kidnap. A person who is visibly in Condition White is easy to kidnap no matter how big and strong. If you look alert and suspicious, you are in less danger.

Visible jewelry: Crooks might not be able to distinguish a Brioni suit from a Men's Wearhouse number, but they can recognize a Rolex. Additionally, big diamond rings stand out. You bought the jewelry to enjoy, but common sense says you should enjoy it carefully.

The car you drive: Do you drive a Lexus or a Chevy Suburban? A Porsche or a Geo Metro? Obviously more conservative cars help, but only to a small extent. A female deputy sheriff in one incident was kidnapped and murdered for a Chevy van. A local celebrity's wife was kidnapped and murdered for a red Cadillac. In both cases they were chosen as targets of opportunity, because they looked like victims, not because of their cars. The young woman in the drive-through line at the beginning of this chapter was murdered for her car, a Camaro, simply because the goblin's stolen car ran out of gas, her car was the first available, and she looked vulnerable. She could have been in any kind of car. A local woman was murdered for a Mazda 626, a very ordinary automobile.

Ex-husbands, -wives, and other stalkers: Women seem to be in the most danger from ex-husbands and lovers—for example, Nicole Brown Simpson. Stalkers of these types are the most difficult to defend against, because in many instances, you are required to deal with them in some respects. Taking every precaution is mandatory if you think you're being stalked. Some stalkers stalk their victims for years before attacking them. All anti-kidnapping techniques must be used for a long period of time in such cases, and this makes it easier on the goblin. Getting the police involved usually just results in the police knowing whom to arrest after the stalker has killed his victim. Tougher anti-stalking laws are helping, but not enough. It is very difficult to prove stalking, and stalkers are relentless. Allowed out on bail, for example, they resume stalking despite court orders and police threats. Remaining vigilant constantly is draining. Eventually you make a mistake. When in combat, I always felt safer moving through the boonies than stationary at fire bases. And I was right. Eventually the sentries would fall asleep, and the NVA, our goblins, would choose that night to attack. When we were sneaking around in their territory in Cambodia, we could sneak up on their sentries, too.

Your job: Bank presidents are more likely victims than day laborers. I got started in the anti-kidnapping area because of a client who was a bank president and thus had anti-kidnapping insurance. He came to me because of a requirement for a trunk survival kit (see below). If you're in such a position, you have to do all of the anti-kidnapping techniques all of the time. The good news is you can afford to. The bad news is you can't afford not to. The survival rate of kidnapees is not good enough to trust to ransom insurance. You have to avoid the kidnapping, period. If you are in such a position, you can afford to take the time and money to get proper training, both in self-defense and anti-terrorist, anti-kidnap driving techniques. You will be most resistant to taking such training because it will take time away from your business, but your business can do without you for a week or two a lot better than your business and family can do without you permanently.

The random kidnapping: The rest of us have to worry about goblins choosing ready victims at random, usually women, usually for rape. It doesn't matter whether you look like Sharon Stone and dress like Pamela Anderson or whether you look and dress like Mother Theresa: You're a target for kidnap and rape if you're female. (These days you don't have to be female. A stalker was just arrested for stalking and planning to rape Steven Spielberg.) You have it easier than the bank president, because your attacker is likely to be stupid, and all you have to be is smart and alert. You probably should also be armed and trained. A serial killer in Houston in the '70s (who is due to be released from prison in the future!) killed a martial arts expert among his victims. Despite what they tell you in martial arts training, there are people too big and too strong to be overwhelmed by a 110-pound person with some martial arts training, and certainly not one in Condition White. Your attacker might be a martial artist, too.

O.K., You've Been Kidnapped Anyway; Now What Do You Do?

A woman came out of a country and western club at closing time. She had left her purse with her gun, a cheap, five-shot Charter Arms .38 special, in it in the trunk. As she retrieved it from the trunk, a man grabbed her from behind, stuck a gun in her back, and said, "Get in. I'll drive." He shoved her into the passenger seat and took her keys and drove. She had the purse on the right side of the passenger seat. He was holding a .357 magnum revolver on her head. She reached into the purse and got a firing grip on her revolver. But she was thinking, This can't be happening to me! This is a dream! It made her hesitate. Anyway he had a gun on her. Maybe he won't hurt me! she thought.

He drove her to a deserted house on a dark road and stopped.

"Get out and leave your clothes!"

She hesitated, not because of what he thought she was hesitating for, but because she was afraid to do what she had to do.

"I said get out, bitch, and leave your clothes!" He reached back inside, his left hand grabbing her upper left arm.

She stopped hesitating and produced her revolver, emptying it into him at contact range. Two shots hit him in the chest, two in the back as he twisted and pulled back to get out of the car. The fifth shot missed as he fell to the ground.

She drove away and called the police from a friend's house. The police found him dead.

In reconstructing the incident, she handled the situation as well as possible once she was kidnapped. The mistake was going to the parking lot in Condition White alone at closing.

She also had a weapon. Without a weapon she would not have acted soon enough to escape, and escape would have been problematic. Jumping out of the car while it was going slowly, for example, might or might not have worked, and she would have been injured hitting the pavement. That also wouldn't incapacitate the goblin, so he could turn around and chase her, now injured.

But she kept her cool enough to survive. If you're kidnapped, so must you. You can't fall apart, unless falling completely apart is part of the plan to distract him. Women who have gone completely "crazy" have sometimes scared off their attackers. Losing control of one's bodily functions in the course of a seizure makes one less desirable as a rape target.

A small woman can do one thing to a big rapist: She can gouge his eyes out. Some self-defense schools teach attacking the groin, but men protect their groin areas, and they expect attacks there. However, pretending to submit, caressing his face, and then gouging his eyes out will usually cause him to lose interest in the rape.

What if you're kidnapped for money, not rape? That's more difficult. The usual suggestions to try to humanize yourself to your captors applies. Talk to them. Try to get them to see you as a human being. With some of the drug-brain-damaged goblins out there, it's far from a sure thing.

Fasten Your Seat Belt

If he's driving, fasten your seat belt and look for an opportunity to cause a crash. He probably won't fasten his seat belt. You will have only one opportunity. Grabbing and deflecting the wheel to cause a medium-speed offset head-on collision is ideal, such as a 30 to 40 mph head-on in which the driver's side of your car hits the driver's side of another vehicle. If he is unbelted, he will, on a non air-bag–equipped car, be killed or at least incapacitated. If he is in the average air bag-equipped car, his legs will be broken in several places, and he will be trapped in the car. Head injuries are also likely. It won't be a walk in the park for you, but you should be in good enough shape to open the right door and exit the car.

If he has you drive, which has happened, fasten your seat belt, appear to follow his instructions, and, as soon as possible, veer sharply into a parked car on his side, trying for a 40 to 50 percent offset collision on his side at 30 mph or greater. Again, if he is unbelted and there is no right-side air bag, he will be killed or incapacitated. If there is an air bag, he will be stunned at best, and most likely trapped in the car with broken legs. If he was out of position at the time of the crash, sitting sideways, for example, in order to keep the gun on you, he might be too close to the air bag and be killed by it.

In timing the crash, whether he is driving or he's a passenger, try to do it while he is talking. People have a tendency to want to finish their sentences. This will slow his response. He's unlikely to shoot you while you are driving anyway because no matter how stupid he is, shooting the driver of the vehicle you're in while at speed is too stupid to be contemplated.

The Trunk Survival Kit

In case you are thrown into the trunk, a trunk survival kit is a good idea. Taped to the top of the front of the trunk, where you might be able to get to it, should be a sharp sheath knife, one you can pull out of its sheath with your hands taped or tied behind your back, and use to cut the tape off. Duct tape is the best thing for "tying" someone up these days that's readily available to the public. Big cable ties are good, too. You have to cut both off. Taped next to the knife should be a handcuff key. Handcuff keys work on all handcuffs. Gun stores sell handcuff keys. I've also found them in mail-order catalogs for places like US Cavalry Store, 1-888-88USCAV. If you're too embarrassed to go to one, or if you live in the Peoples Democratic Republic of New York, get a cop to get you one. If you're a target for kidnapping, you'll have cops or at least security guards working for you or your firm sometime or another.

Now that you've managed to untape or uncuff yourself, what are you going to do?

You need an inside trunk release. If your car has a remote trunk release, this should be no problem. A competent shop should be able to put an additional switch in the trunk. A car stereo or car alarm shop should be able to do that.

Once you've freed yourself you need more tools, first a good flashlight. Putting a Streamlight or Magcharger in so it's perpetually charging is reasonable. The new mini "Combat" lights using lithium batteries are perfect; Streamlight makes one. Laser Products makes a series that will fit in a pocket. Otherwise, a Maglight with batteries changed whenever you change your oil will work.

You should also install an ignition or fuel shut-off switch there. Again, a car alarm place should be able to fit that. The trick is, when the car comes to a stop for a traffic light, etc., shut off the fuel. The bad guys will, quite likely, abandon the car. On the other hand, if you shut off the fuel at a deserted intersection (and how can you tell from the trunk?) the goblins might just decide to eliminate you as a witness and shoot you in the trunk or take you out of the trunk to put you in another vehicle.

At this point you might want to consider having a weapon in the trunk; as powerful a handgun as you can handle should be part of the kit and stowed so you can reach it when in the trunk—don't store it under the spare tire. If handguns are illegal and shotguns are legal in your part of the world, consider a shotgun with an 18.5-inch barrel and, if legal, a folding stock to make it a little easier to handle in the trunk.

Coming out of the trunk with a pistol should solve the problem in your favor. Coming out of the trunk with just wit and good charm probably won't.

Since you might have to shoot from the trunk, a set of earplugs is a good idea. Shooting from inside an enclosed steel container is incredibly loud and will permanently damage your ears. (Do take out the earplugs before the police arrive.) Some cars, including mine, have fold-down rear seats—controlled from the trunk. Flip a switch, fold down the left-side rear seat, and shoot the kidnappers at a traffic light. This will solve the problem, but will make a mess of your expensive car's interior. On the other hand, I wouldn't suggest asking them to step outside so as not to bleed on your car.

Don't shoot them at 80 mph. If you don't believe in guns or can't get one because you live in New York or someplace like that, you should have a cellular phone in your trunk survival kit. As of January 1, 1998, you no longer have to pay for access just to have the ability to dial 911 on an analog (not digital) phone. So you can put an old cell phone in there without paying for monthly access fees. The problem with that, with any battery-operated item of equipment, is that batteries degrade when not in use. Odds are that cellular phone won't work when you need it. Additionally, the trunk is shielded, and if the antenna is on the phone inside the trunk, range and reception are unlikely to be good enough to work. Test and see. If it doesn't, this means mounting a phone that is plugged into the car's electrics and attached to an external antenna. Obviously, only serious kidnap targets are likely to go to all of this trouble and expense.

Even if you have the gun, the cellular phone is a good idea. Even if you have the cellular phone, the gun is a good idea. All of this might not work. You might be so trussed up you can't get free. You might be thrown into the trunk of their car. Carrying a small knife in your sock or shoe, wearing a belt with a handcuff key belt buckle, or carrying a backup weapon on an ankle holster might help. The basic rule is, it's easier to avoid a kidnapping than to escape from one.

CHAPTER EIGHT

DEFEATING MURPHY

Murphy's law rules in all things. Whatever can go wrong will go wrong. All of the corollaries apply, too. It will go wrong in the worst possible way, at the worst possible time, and in the worst possible place. Mr. Murphy, or as we called him, General Murphy, cannot be totally defeated, only held at bay, waiting for the first chance to strike. Any weakness is General Murphy's target.

Maintenance

Just as God rewards the racing teams with the best preparation, he generally ensures the best maintained cars break down less than badly maintained cars. Over the years I've talked to several people who have gotten really high mileage out of their cars with reliability. They had several things in common:

They all changed their oil too much. Modern late '90s cars can go 10–15,000 miles between oil changes, depending on the manufacturer's schedule, and changing oil more often than necessary wastes oil and money and creates a disposal problem. But the guys who got the high miles, 200,000, 300,000 miles, even over 1,000,000 miles a couple of times, changed their oil at 3,000-mile intervals. It gave them a chance to look under the hood and under the car for things wrong. If you make sure a real mechanic with a profit motive looks at your car every 10–15,000 miles, he'll find the frayed fan belt, cracked caliper, bursting hose, or ballooning tire.

Then the key is to do what he says: fix it. Keep fresh fluids, clean filters, and good belts and hoses, and you're ahead of the game. Don't let the tires get to the wear bands because they're less likely to stick in the rain and more likely to get punctured and strand you. Replace ordinary radiator hoses with silicone hoses. They'll last the life of the car, and then all you have to do is check them, not worry about replacing them again.

Replace brake fluid every other year or more often. Old brake fluid causes a slow degradation of braking performance, so slow you won't notice it. Then one day you'll need maximum braking, and the old fluid will have picked up enough water to boil, losing your brakes when you need them the most.

Brake pads should be the best available for the car, carbon metallic or the equivalent. With some brands of cars the best available is OEM. With others it's a high-performance alternative. With Ford Mustangs, for example, the competition pads lasted longer, stopped better, and cost less than the stock pads.

Transmissions should be serviced at least as often as the service schedule requires, perhaps twice as often for an urban warrior. I did see a lot of high mileage cars with transmission troubles in a brand not known for transmission failures. In all cases the very particular owners were over-maintaining the cars, which is normally good. But they checked their transmissions for fluid levels often—with shop rags. Whenever they wiped the transmission fluid off the dipstick and reinserted the dipstick, they were introducing lint from the rag into the transmission. This caused premature failures. Use your fingers to wipe down the dipstick.

Radiators should be serviced at least every other year, too. Coolant failures such as blown hoses are the most common cause of vehicle failures.

There's no magic. It takes work and money to keep a car on the road reliably for years, but with the danger of being attacked if you're stuck on the side of a road, especially at night, you simply must keep the car in safe condition. This goes double for women. A woman on the side of the road for over half an hour, statistically, is in a lot of danger.

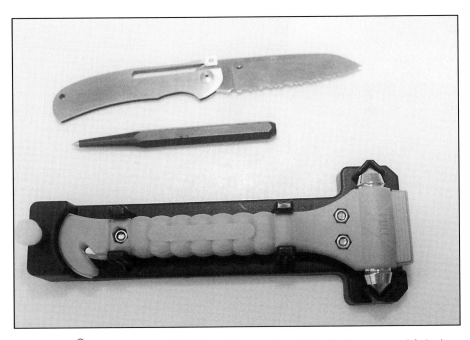

The Life Hammer® will break side (not windshield) glass and cut jammed seat belts. Lacking that, a centerpunch for breaking glass and a serrated-edge pocket knife for cutting jammed seat belts will suffice. These tools will help get you or someone else out of a car that is underwater or on fire—if you don't panic.

Safety Equipment

The Survival Kit

You need an anti-kidnapping survival kit in the trunk, but you also need a survival kit for other emergencies. I used to keep a paramedic knife in the console to cut open jammed seat belts after car accidents—so far it's only been used for someone else's seat belt in someone else's car. I also kept a center punch for punching open the side window glass in case the car is under water.

Recently, I've replaced both of these tools with a Life Hammer®, a small neon-orange tool that combines two heavy, conical steel points that will quickly shatter a side window (not a laminated windshield). The other end holds a recessed razor-sharp blade for cutting through seat belts in one quick motion. Thus, if you're trapped underwater or upside down in a car with jammed doors, you can free a jammed seat belt and break a window to escape. Mount it somewhere where it's as accessible as possible, preferably by both front seat passengers. The center console, if it's big enough, is good. The glovebox usually isn't a good idea; there's too much stuff there. Under the dash works. The hammer comes with a screw-in plastic mount and has a white luminous marker so you can find it in the dark in smoke.

If you do manage to find yourself underwater, remember that panic kills, not the water. The water will come in slowly unless a window is broken, and there will usually be an air pocket at the highest point of the car. External pressure will keep the doors from opening until the pressure equalizes, meaning the interior is almost full of water. If you can't break a window with a centerpunch or Life Hammer, wait for the pressure to equalize, then open the door. There will be a rush of water as you open the door, so take a deep breath before you open it. Likewise, if you do have a tool to break the window, fill your lungs before using it.

If you're at any depth, and you've been breathing inside the car, you've inhaled air compressed by the water pressure. As you go up, that air will expand. If it is in your lungs, it will have to go somewhere, and an embolism will result. This is extremely dangerous. The key is simply to exhale as you go up. Every scuba diver knows this and has had to do an out-of-air ascent from at least 15 feet; expert divers are required to ascend from deeper, and instructors from 60 feet. Just exhale slowly as you kick to the surface.

Checklist for underwater escape
1. Don't panic.
2. Remove seat belt.
3. Remove shoes, restrictive or heavy clothing, anything that can weigh you down as you try to escape.
4. Take a deep breath. Take several if there's air and time.

5. If you have a Life Hammer or centerpunch, use it to break the most convenient side glass. When attempting to break glass, aim for a spot near the base. It will be easier to break there. (This tip came from SWAT officer Sam Woolf, who, in the course of his job, has broken a lot of glass.) If you can't break the side glass, sit as calmly as possible until the vehicle fills with water enough to equalize pressure so you can open the car door.
6. Go out that window or open door and kick to the surface. Exhale constantly as you ascend.
7. Don't panic.

The survival kit is completed by a combat light, a first-aid kit, and a fire extinguisher, with the possible addition of a "car" gun, one that stays in the car (where legal). The fire extinguisher can be in the trunk if you can't find a good place for it. It should, if mounted inside, be mounted low on the floor and securely mounted. You don't need a 10-pound fire extinguisher flying around in a crash.

The fire extinguisher should be a racing quality unit with a metal, not plastic mounting bracket. The best extinguishers are the now hard-to-find Halon 12 units. Halon is the only thing that you can use in an

Halon fire extinguisher mounted accessibly in a safe location. This mounting isn't possible in a lot of cars due to space limitations. The trunk is an acceptable alternative, but then the extinguisher isn't available for a fire in your own car, in most cases. Only fire extinguishers with metal mounts should be mounted inside an automobile. An unrestrained fire extinguisher would be lethal in a crash.

enclosed space and still breathe; it's the only thing that works on passenger aircraft, for example. Naturally, in its infinite wisdom, the federal government made Halon illegal. I've found Halon units still available at racing supply stores, but they're about $100, and if you ever discharge it, I don't know if you'll be able to refill it. But that's the least of my worries if I use a fire extinguisher.

Anything less than 5 B.C. is too small; 10 B.C. is better.

I've only had one chance to use a fire extinguisher, when a truck was on fire. I stopped and asked the owner if he wanted the fire put out. He said yes. Then I discharged the extinguisher and put out the fire. I did ask because no lives were at stake, and some people, knowing how difficult it is to repair a burned-out car, don't want the fire put out until the car is totaled. Repairing a mildly burned car is a horror. The car is never the same electrically. The warranty is voided, and you'll have constant electrical problems.

If you're trapped inside a burning car, however, then you'll want a fire extinguisher, a *big* fire extinguisher. If someone else is trapped in a burning car, and you see them, you'll want a big fire extinguisher. You do not want to watch someone burn. Trust me on this.

If you're really worried about fire, a racing fire bottle system is the solution. Mount a 10-pound unit in the trunk, and put nozzles in the engine compartment and aimed at the driver. This requires professional installation. Doing this under carpeting on a streetworthy car is a job. Some people have a real fear of fire, like some people do about snakes. If you're one of these, remember that fire is, statistically, quite low on the list of things that can kill you in a car.

In the trunk should be a spare tire with air in it (tires normally lose one pound a month. If yours has been in the trunk a long time, it could be flat if you haven't checked it lately), a jack that works, and sufficient tools to change a tire on the side of the road in the dark, including a trouble light. Many women refuse to change tires. Some are physically unable to do the heavy lifting involved, and they're rightfully fearful of getting someone to help them on the side of a lonely road. My red-haired traveling companion told me she would drive on the flat until she reached a place of safety even if the tire and wheel were destroyed. This is O.K., generally, because she drives in civilization, probably not more than five miles from a place of safety. The ability to change a tire, however, should be required for a license. I know of one case in which the driver continued until the wheel was ground away and the brakes damaged. When the caliper was ground away and the brake fluid lost, the vehicle lost braking and crashed. Admittedly, this driver attempted to drive a long way with it.

When I get a new car I'll do a test tire change to see if it presents any problems or needs any kind of special equipment. Some lug wrenches are too short or otherwise poorly designed. Griot's Garage, 1-800-345-5789, sells lug wrenches in both 17 mm and 19 mm form with long enough handles that you don't have to be Hulk Hogan to break the lug nut loose after the kid at NTB decides to try out his new Ingersoll-Rand impact wrench that dishes out 295 lb./ft. of torque.

Other Useful Gadgets
Extra Bright Lights

Standard lights meet legal requirements. There are lights available that may not meet them, but add a lot to your ability to see at night.

First, if you're buying a new car, and they're available, get Xenon headlights if you can. Xenons have twice the brightness of the best quartz halogen lights, and they're daylight spectrum, meaning very white looking at night. The bulbs last 2,500 hours and aren't expensive to replace, but they're expensive units to buy because they have to have a self-leveling unit in them to keep poorly aimed units from blinding on-coming traffic. Don't break one. If it's glass, Griot's Garage, again, sells a 3M film, 20 mils thick, which will protect them from stones on the road, but not someone backing into them.

If you have an old car with stock round or rectangular lights, re-place them with European quartz halogen lights. They're expensive compared to $5 stock units, but $40 to $75 each isn't unreasonable when you see how much extra light they put out.

The expert on lighting is Gene Henderson at Competition Limit-ed, 313-464-1458. Gene is a legend in the U.S. rally scene and knows all there is to know about lighting. Unhappy with American spec. halogen bulbs, he had some made that were higher wattage. I im-mediately bought some and told all my friends to. The problem was the headlight designers, knowing there was no high-wattage alter-native, didn't make their housings to take the extra heat, and I melt-ed the housings and wiring on four headlights on two cars. So if you have a 9000 series bulb, 9004, 9005, 9006, 9007, etc., talk to Gene before just ordering the bulbs. He has relay and wiring kits to adapt to some cars.

European cars, however, with European spec. lights, should be adaptable to high-wattage bulbs. High-wattage bulbs are available in Europe, and, though illegal over there, are widely used. So most of the cars are wired with hefty enough wiring to handle the load, and the headlight fixtures are tough enough to take the extra heat. Putting in a bigger fuse should be all that's required. European bulbs are the H se-ries, H-1, -2, -3, -4, and -7 being examples. H-4 bulbs are a dual filament bulb. Stock is 60/55. A good replacement would be 100/80. 130/100, de-signed for rallying, are certainly bright, but they are hard on the wiring and reflectors and don't last very long.

European cars generally have better-designed headlights than

American or Japanese cars. Those Autobahns with no speed limits and Autoroutes with speed limits enforced only spottily have made for fast drivers. They need the light.

Fog lights usually use H-1, H-2, or H-3 bulbs. Replace them with 100-watt bulbs if it's feasible, but remember, fog lights aren't designed for long-range illumination, they're designed to cut under fog. Fog lights are normally mounted low to facilitate that. On a lot of cars fog lights won't even come on when the high beams are on. (One of my first modifications is usually to put in a relay allowing the fog lights to stay on with the high beams.)

If you're looking for high-speed illumination, and your fog lights are of a stock size, you can replace the lenses with the driving light lens for the same model. If they're faired-in OEM units, you won't have that option.

Normally, I change the high beams to 100 watts, sometimes more if I can, and the low beams I leave at 55 watts if I have good fog lights to use as fill-in lights. If you're in an area with a lot of fog, leave the fogs aimed as fog lights. It's not often a problem where I am.

Auxiliary lights used to be the thing to do, but a lot of bumpers don't make provisions for adding extra lights now. The bumpers are plastic, and often there's no solid mounting point, which makes it difficult to mount extra lights. PIAA makes lights that are small and powerful, and smaller lights are easier to mount sturdily. The purpose of the extra lights is multifold. Obviously, the primary reason is to be able to see better at night. Whether you're just trying to drive fast and don't want to overdrive your headlights or you need to be able to see better to outrun a pursuer, extra lights are good. They can also be used as a weapon to blind an assailant, for example, at a roadblock.

High-wattage backup lights are useful, too, both to illuminate the way when you're doing an evasive maneuver in reverse, and, if switchable from the cockpit, to blind someone following, or just to tell a tailgater to back off a bit. Fifty-five-watt backup bulbs are available to fit most backup light sockets. They might require higher amp fuses, however, and they tend to burn out much more often than standard backup lights.

All high-wattage bulbs burn out more often than standard, so carry spares. I've mounted a couple of mirrors in the garage so I can see all of the bulbs on the car and periodically check them all.

Somewhere in the car should be a first-aid kit. It can be in the trunk. Some cars come with pretty good first-aid kits, but the Japanese first-aid kits are inadequate. The first-aid kit should be up to your capabilities at giving first-aid. When we did One Lap of America, flight paramedic Mad Mac Atteberry brought enough stuff to match his outstanding capabilities. Space was at a premium, but we made room.

If you don't have an inside trunk release, and maybe if you do, there should be a crowbar in the trunk. US Cavalry Store, 1-888-88USCAV, has, of all things, a titanium crowbar, former Russian military issue, weighing only four pounds. Aside from getting you out of the trunk someday, it can be used to pry a bent fender out of a tire so you can drive away from an accident.

A brake light cutoff switch and a taillight cutoff switch are useful in chase situations but increasingly difficult to install on modern cars with anti-lock brakes, traction control, and multiplexed wiring.

A locking gas cap or gas cap door is a must, not to prevent gasoline theft, but to prevent vandalism. Pouring the right stuff into someone's tank and following him until the car stops isn't too far-fetched a scenario. It happened to me once, but the car didn't die, it just wouldn't start. When it was towed in, the mechanic discovered the fuel filter clogged, and further investigation showed the tank to have a couple of pounds of potting soil in it. The culprit's goal was to cost me some aggravation and money, which she did.

Your car's alarm should be state of the art. Most cars come with some alarm these days. If it doesn't do enough, have it upgraded. It should have a radio remote with anti-cloning technology so that someone with a code capture box can't steal the code and thus open the car. (Your garage-door opener should have the same technology.) It should also have a panic button, which will set off the alarm when pushed. In 1995 a woman used her panic button to scare off an attacker in a parking lot. He was caught some hours later and turned out to be wanted for rape and murder. The panic button should not shut off the ignition or fuel. The car should be startable while the panic feature is activated so you can leave the parking lot with the alarm going full blast. Shock sensors, which will set off the alarm when the sensor "hears" the noise of someone trying to break the glass, and anti-towing inclinometers are useful items to have. The alarm should shut off the ignition and/or fuel when armed, and it should be so reliable that it isn't a problem. An alarm that has shut off the ignition but can't be turned off because it's defective is obviously not a good idea.

High-Performance Items

If you're ordering a car and it's an option to have the "performance" or "handling" or "sport" suspension, get it. If there is a heavy-duty radiator, order it, ditto heavy-duty battery, higher performance tires, wider wheels. In the "old" days, we would buy cars then replace the tires with Michelin radials, the wheels with something an inch or so wider, the headlights with quartz halogen European units, the shock absorbers with Konis or Bilsteins, and the brake pads and shoes with semi-metallic units (the best we could get was disc in the front, drums in the back, a combination that was obsolete by 1963 but still pursued today by car companies on the cheap).

Now, at least, you can get a car out of the box that's ready to go. When ordering, things to look for still include high-performance tires. If you don't order the right tires, a new Camaro Z-28 can come governed to 104 mph, for example. Traction control is worth spending money on. Electronic Stability Programs, also known as Electronic Yaw Control and the like, are also useful. If you're being chased, having a car as idiot-proofed as possible helps, because it's very easy to make a serious mistake when scared half to death and driving over your head. (Actually the goal is to drive over *his* head and lose him.)

It generally isn't possible or necessary to order heavy-duty components on European cars. With exceptions, they already come properly equipped for hard driving. The Autobahns demand it.

But if they're available, HD radiator, oil cooler, HD radiator hoses, stainless-steel brake lines, HD power steering or power steering coolers (synthetic power steering fluid), and the like should be on your car.

If you're really in harm's way, and these days who isn't, having the door panel insulation replaced with ballistic quality Kevlar or Spectra, lining the seats with Kevlar or Spectra, and putting Kevlar or Spectra behind the rear seat will help if you're shot at. "Bulletproofing" a car costs at least $100,000 for rifle ammunition, $45,000 for pistol ammunition. The extra weight makes it difficult to maneuver or escape with the car. But judicious use of Kevlar or Spectra will offer some protection in a carjacking attempt or car-to-car shooting. The weak point is still the glass, and replacing it with bullet-resistant glass is cost prohibitive. Kevlar or Spectra, properly used, won't increase the weight significantly. If it replaces existing insulation, it might not increase the weight at all.

Wearing a bulletproof vest while driving is not an unreasonable idea. Many of the "saves" in the Second Chance catalog are police officers who were involved in car wrecks, and the Kevlar vest protected them from thoracic trauma. A Level 2 vest, which, with modern construction, is almost thin enough to be semi-comfortable in some climates, will defeat virtually any handgun you're likely to encounter and will increase your chances of survival in an accident. If I lived in an area that didn't allow law-abiding citizens to carry a weapon, I would wear a vest all the time. The crime rate in such places justifies it. Washington, D.C., with the most restrictive gun laws in the United States, is probably the most dangerous place to live in the United States.

CHAPTER NINE

PUTTING IT ALL TOGETHER

We've spent a lot of time talking about how to stay out of trouble while using an automobile. The skills involve situational awareness, the combat mindset, traffic skills, driving skills, and tactics. Dr. Ignatius Piazza, a shooting instructor and founder of Front Sight Academy, decribed four levels of competence (but doesn't claim to have invented the concept):

- Unconsciously Incompetent: The UI is incompetent but does not know he is incompetent because he has had no training or poor training, and has not yet experienced a situation that would clearly demonstrate his inadequacies.
- Consciously Incompetent: If the UI survives his first lesson, and is smart enough to place the blame on the man in the mirror, the UI automatically graduates to the level of CI. The CI now knows he does not know and seeks help in acquiring the proper skills in the use of his weapon (in this case, your car).
- Consciously Competent: With proper training and practice, the CI develops into the CC.
- Unconsciously Competent: This is the goal. Only very motivated and dedicated students reach this level. The UC functions flawlessly even under stressful situations because the UC's extensive training overrides his conscious thought process.

If you take Dr. Piazza's four levels of competency and apply them to driving automobiles in the modern world, it's obvious that most of the people out there, 99 percent, are Unconsciously Incompetent in all of the aforementioned skills. Very few are Unconsciously Competent in any or all of them. If you do nothing but read this book, you'll become Consciously Incompetent in most of the skills and Consciously Competent in a few. You can get skills in situational awareness, the Color Code, and basic accident avoidance from reading (and rereading) parts of this book and taking them to heart. But you can't learn high-performance driving from a book. You can learn the basic evasive techniques by reading the book and then practicing them, assuming you can find a place where it's possible. To go past Consciously Incompetent in high-performance driving, you'll need training. It's a big commitment. If you spend a week a year, half your vacations, in training, you'll need a few years to become Consciously Competent. Becoming Unconsciously Competent is a matter of motivation, and that takes time and dedication, weekly practices as well as attending more than one school, monthly autocrosses or track sessions, and attending more than one driving school. I'm not vain enough to overcredit what you can get from a book. The rest is up to you. But the big thing, situational awareness, the Color Code, you can learn from a book, and by now you should have. If one reader remembers Condition Yellow and spots someone following him home and calls the police instead of going home, if one woman sees someone loitering about her car at a mall and asks a security guard for an escort and avoids the goblin, if one driver avoids a stupid, fatal accident because of something he read in this book, then it has been worthwhile.

INDEX

Accidents
   Avoiding, 22–39
   Steering around, 33
Air bags, 42, 43, 45, 93, 94, 113
Alarms, car *See* Security systems
American Pistol Institute *See* Gunsite Training Center
Anti-lock brakes, maximizing, 27–33
   Practice exercises, 27–31
Army training, 5–7, 10, 11, 17, 18, 37, 40, 72
Autocrossing, 7, 9, 59
Ayoob, Massad, 10, 73
Bob Bondurant School of High Performance Driving
   See Driving Schools
Bolin, Nils, 50
Bondurant, Bob, 8 *See also* Driving schools
Braking, 53–55
British Royal Automobile Club, 70
Buff, Bill, 8, 24
Bulletproof vest, 124
Bulletproofing, 124
Car, as weapon, 18
Carjacking, avoiding, 102–110
Cellular phones, 38, 104, 115
Chapman, Ray, 10
Chased, being, 77, 78 *See also* Followed, being
Clark, Jimmy, 53, 56
Combat concepts, 17–21
Combat elements, 17, 18
   Mindset, 17, 18
   Tactics, sound, 18
   Weapons, 18
Competence, levels of, 125
Competition Limited, 121
Concentration, 68
Cooper, Jeff, 10, 12–16
Cornering, 53, 54, 56–59
   Apex, definition of, 56
   Apex, early, 57
   Apex, late, 57
   Exiting, 58
Courtesy, 67
Cut-off switches, 114, 123
Davis, Richard, 73

Daytime running lights (DRLs), 36 *See also* Lights
Dead pedal, 41
Discipline, 19
Driving schools, 59–64, 99, 100
   Bob Bondurant School of High Performance Driving, 29, 31, 33, 42, 59, 60–63, 99, 100
   Car Guys, Inc., 64
   Derek Daly Racing School, 63
   Dodge/Skip Barber Driving School, 61, 62
   Driving Dynamics, 24, 63
   Skip Barber Racing School, 61, 62
   Sports Car Club of America, 60
Driving, invisible, 20, 21, 37, 71, 72
Driving, techniques, evasive, 72–100
Evasive maneuvers, 80–100
   Bootlegger hairpin, 80–86
   Moonshiner's turn, 86–90
   Pursuit line, 90, 91
   Racing line, 91
   Traffic line, 91, 92
   Contact, making, 92–99
   Running off road, 93–95
   Roadblocks
      Single-vehicle, 96, 97
      Two-vehicle, 97–99
   High speeds, 99
   Curbs, jumping, 99
   Training, 99, 100
Fire extinguisher, 119, 120
First-aid kits, 119, 122
Flashlights, 106, 114
Followed, being, 74, 75 *See also* Chased, being
Followed, preventing, 104
Four-wheel drifts, 52
Front Sight Academy, 125
G-forces, measuring, 31, 32
G-Meter, 32
Garage door openers, 107, 108, 123
Gas caps, locking, 123
"Gizmo," 85
Griot's Garage, 121
Guns *See* Weapons
Gunsite Training Center, 10, 13

Gurney, Dan, 62
Haywood, Hurley, 69
High-performance driving techniques, 40–64
    Smoothness, 53–56
High-performance items, 123, 124
Horn, 69
International Practical Shooting Confederation (IPSC), 9
Intersection crashes, avoiding, 34, 35
Intimidation driving, 35
Kidnapping, 110–115
Lights, 36, 121, 122 See also Daytime running lights
Mace, 108
Maintenance, car, 116, 117
McCluggage, Denise, 24, 55
Median, crossing, 25, 26
Mercedes-Benz, 27, 32, 33, 106, 107
Mirrors, alignment, 22–25
Mirrors, vanity, using, 75
Moss, Stirling, 58
National Motorists Association, 24
O'Connell, Johnny, 8
Oversteer, 50–52
Panic control, 72–74
Paul, John, 8
Pepper spray, 108
Piazza, Ignatius, 125
Porsche Club of America, 9, 32, 59
Posture, correct, 41, 42, 44
Radar Reporter, 24
Railroad tracks, 38
Rearview mirrors See Mirror, alignment
Red lights, running, 34, 35
Road rage, 66, 70
Rutherford, John, IV, 8
Safety equipment, 118–121
    Life Hammer®, 117, 118
Seat belts, 38, 113
Seat belts, as performance tool, 48–50
Second Chance Body Armor Company, 73
Security systems, 106

Senna, Ayrton, 33, 36, 56
Shelby, Carroll, 62
Sitting, in car, 41, 42, 44
Situational awareness, color codes, 12–16
    Condition white, 14
    Condition yellow, 14, 15
    Condition orange, 15, 16
    Condition red, 16
Situational awareness, using, 33–35
Skids, rear-wheel, 50–52
Spin control, 52, 53
Sports Car Club of America (SCCA), 6, 8, 9, 59, 60, 63
Steering techniques, 43, 46, 47
Steering wheel, hand position, 42, 43, 45
Stewart, Jackie, 55
Stopping distances
    Cutting in half, 32, 33
Stun gun, 108, 109 See also Weapons
Sullivan, Danny, 53
Survival kit See Safety equipment
Tail, losing, 75–77
Tailgaters, getting rid of, 68, 69
Tailgating, avoiding, 25
Texas World Speedway, 53
Tires, changing, 120, 121
Training, 18, 19
Trunk releases, 114, 123
Trunk survival kit, 113, 114
Two-second rule, 25, 34
U-turns, 26, 27
Understeer, 50, 51
Underwater escape, 118, 119
Unser, Johnny, 8
Valentine Research G-Analyst, 30
Volvo, 50
Ward, Roger, 49
Weapons, 18, 108, 109, 114, 115, 119
Weather, bad, 39
Weight transfer, 51